Betty Crocker's

RED SPOON COLLECTION™

BEST RECIPES FOR FISH AND SHELLFISH

PRENTICE HALL

New York London Toronto Sydney Tokyo Singapore

Prentice Hall
15 Columbus Circle
New York, New York 10023

Published simultaneously in Canada by Prentice Hall Canada Inc.

Library of Congress Cataloging-in-Publication Data

Best recipes for fish and shellfish.—1st ed.
    p. cm.—(Betty Crocker's Red Spoon collection)
    Includes index.
    1. Cookery (Fish) 2. Cookery (Shellfish) I. Series
TX747.B419 1990
641.6'92—dc20   89-8416
                                       CIP

Manufactured in the United States of America

10 9 8 7 6 5 4 3 2 1

First Prentice Hall Edition

Front Cover: Shrimp Étouffée

CONTENTS

INTRODUCTION 5

1 APPETIZERS AND FIRST COURSES 7

2 STEWS, CHOWDERS AND BISQUES 20

3 SOUFFLÉS AND OMELETS 32

4 SALADS AND SANDWICHES 43

5 FIN FISH 60

6 SHELLFISH 81

RED SPOON TIPS 97

INDEX 109

INTRODUCTION

Seafood can figure into any and every meal. Breakfast with Scrambled Eggs with Smoked Salmon (page 33), lunch with a simple tuna sandwich and dinner with steamed lobster and drawn butter all appeal to diners everywhere. For brunch, a Crabmeat Frittata (page 42) or for cocktails a snack of Caviar Canapés (page 16) can provide elegance and variety like no other kind of food. Although Americans historically have been less enthusiastic fish eaters than, for example, Scandinavians (who consume six times as much fish per person), we're beginning to catch up. Today even landlocked folks can enjoy fish, not only from local lakes and streams but also from countries as far away as New Zealand. Two additional reasons for this burgeoning popularity are versatility and healthfulness.

Fish can be cooked in every conceivable way: poached or steamed, deep fried or pan fried, baked, grilled, broiled or smoked, plunked on a plank or wrapped in a parchment envelope. And, fish is truly good for you, low in calories and high in protein. Easy to digest and naturally tender, fish cooks quickly no matter what method you use. Here's a brief rundown on some techniques:

POACHING: A perfect method for gently cooking lean fish (see Sole with Red Grapes, page 60), poaching can also add flavor to fatty fish such as salmon (see Salmon with Creamy Cucumber Salsa, page 70). Be sure your pan is large enough; a poacher that spans two standard stove burners is ideal for whole fish. If you don't have a removable poaching rack, wrap the fish in cheesecloth so that it doesn't break apart when you remove it from the poaching liquid after cooking. If you must, you can cut the fish in half and reassemble it on a platter for serving. (Disguise the "seam" with a row of thin lemon slices or a sauce.)

STEAMING: Steamed fish is similar to poached fish, but when steamed the fish is held above the cooking liquid rather than immersed in it. Time your cooking from the first emergence of steam from between pan and lid.

BAKING: Fatty fish are the best bakers (see Baked Salmon Steaks, page 71), but lean fish can be baked, provided it is intermittently basted and not overcooked. Leaving head and tail intact keeps the juices in the fish for a moister result. Any fish will benefit from being baked *en papillote,* wrapped in parchment or foil (see Sea Bass in Cilantro, page 69, and Pompano en Papillote, page 64). Planking fish is another baking method. An oiled oak or cedar board is used as the cooking utensil, and it imparts a unique wood flavor to salmon or other oily fish.

BROILING: In the oven or on the grill, broiling is quick and convenient for small whole fish, steaks or fillets. Brush lean fish with oil or melted butter first. Hinged baskets make turning fish on the grill a foolproof procedure. Be sure to oil grills (and baskets) before using.

PANFRYING OR SAUTÉING: Another quick-cooking method, panfrying is especially suited for small fish and fillets. Coat the fish in flour or bread crumbs and fry it in a mixture of butter and oil or butter alone, if you prefer. For variation, try the Stir-fried Fish with Pea Pods (page 78).

DEEP-FRYING: Successful deep-frying depends on the temperature of the oil. Fry only a few pieces at a time—don't crowd the pan—or the oil will cool, causing the fish to absorb oil and become greasy and sodden instead of crisp and crunchy. A frying thermometer will help you maintain an accurate temperature for best results.

SHELLFISH: Lobster, clams, crabs, shrimp and oysters can be boiled, steamed, broiled or fried, and also lend themselves to luxurious stews, chowders and bisques enhanced with vegetables, seasoning and often cream.

Finally, a word about seasonings. Fresh herbs have a natural affinity for fish, as do many spices, wine, cream, mushrooms and onions and their relatives. You'll find nearly a dozen seafood-compatible sauces in the Red Spoon Tips section, perfect for everything from spur-of-the-moment occasions to grand events. This book holds just about all the information you need to know to enjoy fish.

· 1 ·

APPETIZERS AND FIRST COURSES

Parsley Scallops

4 cups water
12 ounces sea scallops
⅓ cup bottled oil and vinegar dressing
3 tablespoons snipped parsley
1 clove garlic, finely chopped

Heat water to boiling in 10-inch skillet; reduce heat. Place scallops in single layer in skillet. Simmer uncovered until scallops can be pierced easily with a fork, about 3 minutes; drain. Cut into bite-size pieces if necessary. Mix remaining ingredients; pour over scallops. Cover and refrigerate about 4 hours, stirring occasionally.

Fried Squid

8 SERVINGS

1 pound cleaned squid
Vegetable oil
½ cup all-purpose flour
2 eggs, slightly beaten
1 cup dry bread crumbs
Salt
Lemon wedges

Cut squid body cones into ½-inch slices; leave tentacles whole. Pat dry.

Heat oil (1 to 1½ inches) to 375°. Coat squid with flour. Dip into eggs; coat with bread crumbs. Fry a few squid pieces at a time until golden brown, 2 to 3 minutes. Drain; sprinkle with salt. Serve with lemon wedges.

Oysters Rockefeller

2 APPETIZERS

Rock salt
12 medium oysters in shells
2 tablespoons finely chopped onion
2 tablespoons snipped parsley
2 tablespoons finely chopped celery
1/4 cup margarine or butter
1/2 cup chopped fresh or frozen spinach,
   partially thawed and drained
1/3 cup dry bread crumbs
1/4 teaspoon salt
7 drops of red pepper sauce
Dash of ground anise

Fill three pie plates, 9 × 1¼ inches, ½ inch deep with rock salt; sprinkle with water. Scrub oysters in shells under running cold water. Break off thin end of shell with hammer. Force a table knife or shucking knife between halves of the shell at broken end; pull apart. Cut oyster at muscle to separate from shell. Remove any bits of shell. Place oyster on deep half of shell; discard other half. Arrange filled shells on rock salt base.

Heat oven to 450°. Cook and stir onion, parsley and celery in margarine until onion is tender. Mix in remaining ingredients. Spoon about 1 tablespoon spinach mixture onto oyster in each shell. Bake 10 minutes.

Stuffed Oysters

1 DOZEN APPETIZERS

12 oysters in shells
1/2 cup clam juice
1/2 cup white wine
Juice of 1 lime
1/4 cup margarine or butter
1 cup dry bread crumbs
1/2 cup toasted sesame seed
1/4 cup bottled herbed vinaigrette salad
   dressing
1/4 cup Casera Sauce (page 83)
1/4 cup snipped parsley
1 tablespoon finely chopped fully cooked
   smoked ham
1 cup shredded Monterey Jack cheese
   (about 4 ounces)

Remove oysters from shells; reserve 12 half shells. Heat clam juice, wine and lime juice to boiling; reduce heat. Simmer uncovered until reduced to 1 cup. Add margarine and oysters. Simmer oysters in clam juice mixture 2 minutes; do not overcook. Remove oysters with slotted spoon; keep warm.

Stir remaining ingredients except cheese into clam juice mixture; mix completely. Divide half the stuffing among shells. Top each with oyster. Cover each with remaining stuffing; sprinkle with cheese. Set oven control to broil and/or 550°. Broil 2 to 3 inches from heat until cheese is melted, 3 to 4 minutes.

Melon and Smoked Salmon

12 SERVINGS

1 cantaloupe, casaba, honeydew or
   Spanish melon (about 3 pounds)
¼ pound thinly sliced smoked salmon, cut
   into 1-inch strips

Cut melon into halves; scoop out seeds and fibers. Cut each half lengthwise into 6 wedges; remove rind. Cut crosswise slits 1½ inches apart in each melon wedge. Place several strips of salmon lengthwise over each wedge; push salmon into slits.

MELON AND SMOKED SALMON BITES: Cut melon into bite-size pieces. Wrap each piece with strip of smoked salmon; secure with wooden picks.

Salmon Pinwheels

ABOUT 45 APPETIZERS

1 tablespoon lemon juice
¾ teaspoon snipped dill or ¼ teaspoon
   dried dill weed
2 packages (3 ounces each) cream cheese,
   softened
3 packages (3 ounces each) sliced smoked
   salmon or 30 pieces sliced smoked
   salmon, each 3 × 2½ inches

Mix lemon juice, dill and cream cheese. Spread about 2½ teaspoons cream cheese mixture on each salmon slice. Roll up, beginning at narrow end. Cut rolls crosswise into 3 pieces.

Do-ahead Tip: After cutting rolls into pieces, cover with damp towel and plastic wrap; refrigerate no longer than 24 hours.

Following pages: Melon and Smoked Salmon, left, and Fried Squid, right (page 7)

Crab and Avocado Cocktail

6 SERVINGS

1 cup cooked crabmeat
2 avocados, cut up
2 jalapeño peppers, seeded and finely chopped
1/4 cup chopped tomato
Juice of 1 lime (about 1/4 cup)
2 tablespoons olive or vegetable oil
2 tablespoons chopped onion
2 tablespoons snipped fresh cilantro
1 clove garlic, finely chopped
3/4 teaspoon salt
Dash of pepper
1 1/2 cups finely shredded lettuce
Lime or lemon wedges

Mix all ingredients except lettuce and lime. Place 1/4 cup lettuce in each of 6 serving dishes. Divide crabmeat mixture among dishes. Garnish with lime.

Anchovy-Garlic Dip

2/3 CUP

2 cans (2 ounces each) anchovy fillets
1/2 cup margarine or butter, softened
2 cloves garlic, cut into halves
Snipped parsley
Vegetable Dippers* or Italian bread sticks

Drain anchovies, reserving 1 tablespoon oil. Place anchovies, reserved oil, the margarine and garlic in blender container. Cover and blend on medium speed, scraping sides of blender frequently, about 1 minute. Garnish with parsley. Serve at room temperature with Vegetable Dippers.

*Carrot sticks, cauliflower or broccoli flowerets, celery sticks, cucumber or zucchini sticks, green onion pieces, small whole mushrooms, red or green pepper strips, radishes with stems.

Fish en Escabeche

1 pound firm white fish fillets (orange
roughy, haddock or mackerel), cut
into ½-inch cubes
⅓ cup lemon juice
⅓ cup lime juice
¼ cup olive or vegetable oil
1 tablespoon snipped fresh cilantro or
1 teaspoon dried cilantro leaves
1 teaspoon snipped fresh oregano or
¼ teaspoon dried oregano leaves
¾ teaspoon salt
¼ teaspoon pepper
12 small pimiento-stuffed green olives
2 jalapeño peppers, seeded and chopped
1 small onion, finely chopped (about
¼ cup)
1 clove garlic, finely chopped
1 large tomato, seeded and chopped
(about 1 cup)
1 avocado, peeled and chopped

Heat ¾ inch water to boiling in 10-inch skillet; carefully place fish in water. Heat to boiling; reduce heat. Simmer uncovered just until fish is opaque, about 30 seconds (do not overcook, or fish will fall apart); drain carefully.

Mix remaining ingredients except tomato and avocado in glass or plastic dish. Gently stir in fish. Cover and refrigerate 2 days, stirring occasionally.

Just before serving, gently stir in tomato and avocado; drain. Serve fish mixture with crackers or tortilla chips, if desired.

Chunky Tuna Salsa

1 can (6½ ounces) tuna, well drained
¾ cup chopped red onion
1 large tomato, chopped
1 jalapeño pepper, seeded and chopped
1 tablespoon lemon juice
Snipped fresh cilantro
Tortilla chips

Break up tuna with fork. Carefully mix tuna and remaining ingredients except cilantro and tortilla chips. Sprinkle with cilantro. Serve with tortilla chips.

Following pages: Fish en Escabeche

Caviar Canapés

10 slices white sandwich bread
1/4 cup margarine or butter, softened
1 green onion, finely chopped
1 jar (2 ounces) black or red caviar

Cut 4 circles from each bread slice with 1½-inch round cutter. Place rounds on ungreased cookie sheet. Set oven control to broil and/or 550°. Broil bread rounds with tops 3 to 4 inches from heat until golden brown, about 1 minute; cool.

Mix margarine and onions; spread over toasted rounds. Top with caviar. Cover and refrigerate until serving time.

Do-ahead Tip: After toasting bread rounds, cover and store at room temperature no longer than 24 hours.

Smoked Fish Appetizers

Smoked Fish Spread (below)
6 slices day-old sandwich bread
Margarine or butter, softened
Sliced almonds
Dill or parsley

SMOKED FISH SPREAD

4 ounces smoked fish, finely chopped
2 tablespoons finely chopped celery
1 tablespoon finely chopped onion
2 teaspoons lemon juice
Dash of pepper
1/4 cup mayonnaise or salad dressing

Prepare Smoked Fish Spread. Trim crusts from bread slices; spread with margarine. Spread bread slices with fish spread. Cut each slice into 3 pieces. Garnish with almonds, dill or parsley.

Mix all ingredients.

Do-ahead Tip: Arrange appetizers on serving plate. Cover with dampened towel; wrap with plastic wrap. Refrigerate no longer than 24 hours.

Crabmeat Puffs

1 package (6 ounces) frozen crabmeat,
thawed, drained, cartilage removed
and chopped
2 packages (3 ounces each) cream cheese,
softened
½ teaspoon salt
¼ teaspoon garlic powder
40 wonton skins
1 egg, slightly beaten
Vegetable oil

Mix chopped crabmeat, cream cheese, salt and garlic powder. Brush wonton skin with egg.

Place heaping teaspoonful crabmeat mixture in center of wonton skin. (Cover remaining skins with dampened towel to keep them pliable.) Top with another wonton skin; press edges to seal. Brush dab of egg on center of each side of puff. Make a pleat on each edge, pressing to seal. Repeat with remaining wonton skins. (Cover puffs with dampened towel or plastic wrap to keep them from drying out.)

Heat vegetable oil (1½ inches) in wok to 350°. Fry 4 to 5 puffs at a time until golden brown, turning 2 or 3 times, about 2 minutes. Drain.

Do-ahead Tip: Prepare Crabmeat Puffs; wrap, label and freeze no longer than 6 weeks. Just before serving, heat frozen puffs uncovered in 400° oven until hot, about 10 minutes. Drain.

Following pages: Crabmeat Puffs, left, and Smoked Fish Appetizers, right

STEWS, CHOWDERS AND BISQUES

Salmon—Wild Rice Soup

6 SERVINGS

3 slices bacon, cut into ¹/₂-inch pieces
1 medium onion, sliced
1 medium stalk celery, thinly sliced
4 ounces mushrooms, sliced
2 tablespoons all-purpose flour
¹/₂ teaspoon dry mustard
¹/₄ teaspoon dried rosemary leaves
1 cup cooked wild rice
2 cans (10³/₄ ounces each) condensed
  chicken broth
1 cup half-and-half
1 can (15¹/₂ ounces) salmon, drained and
  flaked

Cook bacon in 3-quart saucepan until crisp; remove bacon with slotted spoon and reserve. Cook and stir onion, celery and mushrooms in bacon fat until celery is tender. Stir in flour, mustard and rosemary. Cook over low heat, stirring constantly, until bubbly; remove from heat. Stir in wild rice and broth.

Heat to boiling; reduce heat. Cover and simmer 10 minutes. Stir in reserved bacon, half-and-half and salmon. Heat, stirring occasionally, until hot.

Dilled Salmon Chowder

2 medium potatoes, cut into ½-inch
  cubes
2 medium stalks celery, sliced
1 medium carrot, sliced
1 medium onion, chopped
1 can (10¾ ounces) condensed chicken
  broth
1 broth can water
1 tablespoon snipped fresh dill or 1 teaspoon dried dill weed
½ teaspoon salt
¼ teaspoon pepper
2 cups half-and-half
1 can (15½ ounces) salmon, drained and
  flaked

Heat to boiling all ingredients except half-and-half and salmon in 4-quart Dutch oven; reduce heat.

Cover and simmer until vegetables are crisp-tender, about 10 minutes. Stir in half-and-half and salmon; heat until hot.

Fish and Corn Chowder

6 slices bacon, cut into ½-inch pieces
2 cups water
1 teaspoon salt
¼ teaspoon white pepper
1 pound cod, cut into 1-inch pieces
4 new potatoes, cut into ¼-inch slices
2 medium stalks celery, sliced
1 medium onion, chopped
1 can (17 ounces) whole kernel corn,
  undrained
1 cup half-and-half

Cook bacon in Dutch oven until crisp; remove bacon and drain. Drain fat from Dutch oven.

Stir remaining ingredients except half-and-half into Dutch oven. Heat to boiling; reduce heat. Cover and simmer until fish and potatoes are done, 15 to 20 minutes. Stir in half-and-half; heat until hot. Sprinkle each serving with bacon, and if desired, garnish with celery leaves.

Hearty Fish Chowder

2 pounds frozen halibut or haddock
  fillets, thawed
3 cups water
4 medium potatoes, cut into 1/2-inch pieces
  (about 4 cups)
1 large onion, chopped (about 1 cup)
1 medium green pepper, chopped (about
  1 cup)
1 medium tomato, peeled and chopped
  (about 3/4 cup)
1 cup half-and-half
1 teaspoon salt
1/4 teaspoon pepper
1/3 cup shredded Cheddar cheese

Heat halibut fillets and water to boiling in
Dutch oven; reduce heat. Cover and simmer
just until halibut flakes easily with fork, 10 to
15 minutes. (Cooking time varies according to
thickness of halibut.) Remove halibut and broth
from Dutch oven. Flake or cut halibut into
bite-size pieces; reserve broth.

Simmer potatoes, onion and green pepper in
1 cup of the reserved broth just until potatoes
are tender, about 15 minutes. Stir in remaining broth, the halibut, tomato, half-and-half,
salt and pepper. Heat until chowder is hot.
Sprinkle with cheese.

Hot and Sour Fish Soup

2 tablespoons cornstarch
2 tablespoons cold water
1/2 pound fish fillets, cut into 1-inch pieces
3 tablespoons white vinegar
2 teaspoons soy sauce
2 medium carrots, cut into thin strips
2 bottles (8 ounces each) clam juice or
  2 cups fish or chicken broth
1 jar (7 ounces) sliced shiitake mushrooms, undrained
1 to 2 teaspoons red pepper sauce
4 ounces fresh Chinese pea pods or
  1 package (6 ounces) frozen Chinese
  pea pods, thawed

Mix cornstarch and cold water. Mix cornstarch
mixture and remaining ingredients except pepper sauce and pea pods in Dutch oven. Heat
to boiling; reduce heat.

Cover and simmer until fish flakes easily with
fork, 3 to 5 minutes. Stir in pepper sauce and
pea pods.

Creamy Fish Soup with Garlic Toast

4 SERVINGS

1½ cups mayonnaise or salad dressing
3 cloves garlic, finely chopped
¼ cup margarine or butter
8 slices French bread
1 clove garlic, cut into halves
1 pound fish fillets, cut into 1-inch pieces
1½ cups chardonnay or dry white wine
¼ teaspoon salt
6 slices onion
3 slices lemon
5 sprigs parsley
1 bay leaf

Mix mayonnaise and chopped garlic; cover and refrigerate. Heat 2 tablespoons of the margarine in 10-inch skillet over medium heat until melted. Cook 4 of the bread slices in margarine, turning once, until brown; rub one side of toasted bread with garlic half. Repeat with remaining margarine and bread.

Place fish fillet pieces in same skillet. Add remaining ingredients; if necessary, add just enough water to cover fish. Heat to boiling; reduce heat. Simmer uncovered until fish flakes easily with fork, about 6 minutes. Remove fish, using slotted spoon; keep warm.

Strain cooking liquid; return to skillet. Gradually beat in mayonnaise mixture, using wire whisk or spoon. Cook over low heat, stirring constantly, until hot and slightly thickened. Fold in fish. Place 2 slices garlic toast upright in each of 4 soup bowls. Pour soup between slices; sprinkle with paprika, if desired.

New England Chowder

4 SERVINGS

¼ cup cut-up bacon or lean salt pork
1 medium onion, chopped (about ½ cup)
2 cans (6½ ounces each) minced clams, drained (reserve liquid)
1 cup finely chopped potato
½ teaspoon salt
Dash of pepper
2 cups milk

Cook and stir bacon and onion in 2-quart saucepan until bacon is crisp and onion is tender. Add enough water, if necessary, to reserved clam liquid to measure 1 cup. Stir clams, clam liquid, potato, salt and pepper into bacon mixture. Heat to boiling; reduce heat. Cover and boil until potato is tender, about 15 minutes. Stir in milk. Heat, stirring occasionally, just until hot (do not boil).

Following pages: Creamy Fish Soup with Garlic Toast, left, and Hearty Fish Chowder, right

Mediterranean Fish Soup

8 SERVINGS

12 slices French bread, cut ¾ inch thick
2 medium onions, chopped
3 cloves garlic, crushed
¼ cup olive or vegetable oil
3 medium tomatoes, chopped
1 cup clam juice
6 cups water
2 teaspoons salt
1 teaspoon finely chopped fresh thyme or ½ teaspoon dried thyme leaves
½ teaspoon crushed fennel seed
½ teaspoon ground turmeric
⅛ teaspoon pepper
1 bay leaf
2 pounds assorted white fish (halibut, haddock, pollack, red snapper, whiting, bass, cod, flounder)

Place bread in single layer on cookie sheet. Bake in 325° oven until crisp, about 30 minutes. Cook and stir onions and garlic in oil in Dutch oven over medium heat until onions are tender. Add tomatoes, clam juice, water, salt, thyme, fennel seed, turmeric, pepper and bay leaf. Heat to boiling; reduce heat. Cover and cook 5 minutes.

Cut fish into 1-inch chunks; add to tomato mixture. Heat to boiling; reduce heat. Cover and cook until fish flakes easily with fork, about 5 minutes. Remove bay leaf before serving. Serve with French bread.

Manhattan Clam Chowder

5 SERVINGS

¼ cup finely cut-up lean salt pork
1 small onion, finely chopped
2 cans (6½ ounces each) minced or whole clams,* drained (reserve liquid)
2 cups finely chopped potatoes
⅓ cup chopped celery
1 cup water
2 teaspoons snipped parsley
1 teaspoon salt
¾ teaspoon snipped fresh thyme leaves or ¼ teaspoon dried thyme leaves
⅛ teaspoon pepper
1 can (16 ounces) whole tomatoes, undrained

Cook and stir salt pork and onion in Dutch oven until pork is crisp and onion is tender. Stir clam liquid, potatoes, celery and water into onion and pork. Heat to boiling; reduce heat. Cover and boil until potatoes are tender, about 10 minutes. Stir in clams and remaining ingredients; break up tomatoes with fork. Heat to boiling, stirring occasionally.

*1 pint shucked fresh clams with liquid can be substituted for the canned clams. Chop clams and stir in with the potatoes.

Clam Bisque

4 SERVINGS

1 teaspoon grated onion
1 tablespoon margarine or butter
1 tablespoon all-purpose flour
2 teaspoons snipped parsley
1 teaspoon salt
1/8 teaspoon pepper
1/8 teaspoon celery salt
2 cups milk
1 cup water or chicken broth
1 can (6 1/2 ounces) minced clams

Cook and stir onion in margarine over low heat. Stir in flour, parsley, salt, pepper and celery salt. Cook, stirring constantly, until mixture is smooth and bubbly. Remove from heat; stir in milk and water. Heat to boiling, stirring constantly. Boil and stir 1 minute. Stir in clams (with liquid).

OYSTER BISQUE: Substitute 1/2 pint oysters, chopped, and oyster liquid for the clams and clam liquid.

CRAB BISQUE: Substitute 1 can (7 1/2 ounces) crabmeat, chopped, and crabmeat liquid for the clams and clam liquid.

LOBSTER BISQUE: Substitute 1 can (8 ounces) lobster, chopped, and lobster liquid for the clams and clam liquid.

Oyster and Vegetable Chowder

6 SERVINGS

1/3 cup margarine or butter
1 1/2 pints shucked select or large oysters, undrained*
1 package (16 ounces) frozen corn-broccoli mixture
3 1/2 cups milk
1 1/2 teaspoons salt
Dash of pepper

Heat margarine in 3-quart saucepan until melted. Stir in oysters and vegetables. Cook over medium heat, stirring frequently, until edges of oysters are curled and vegetables are done, about 14 minutes.

Stir in milk, salt and pepper. Cook over low heat, stirring frequently, until hot.

*3 cans (8 ounces each) whole oysters, undrained, can be substituted for fresh oysters; stir in with the milk.

Oriental Oyster Stew

4 SERVINGS

1 can (10¾ ounces) condensed chicken
   broth
1 soup can water
2 tablespoons soy sauce
¼ teaspoon grated gingerroot
1 pint shucked select or large oysters,
   undrained
2 cups chopped Chinese cabbage
8 ounces sliced mushrooms
½ cup bean sprouts*
4 green onions (with tops), cut into 1-inch
   pieces

Heat chicken broth, water, soy sauce and
gingerroot to boiling in 3-quart saucepan. Add
oysters, cabbage, mushrooms and bean sprouts.
Heat to boiling; reduce heat. Cover and simmer until cabbage is crisp-tender, about 2 minutes. Garnish with green onions.

*Pea pods can be substituted for the bean
sprouts.

Carolina Crabmeat Soup

6 SERVINGS

2 cups milk
¼ teaspoon mace
2 pieces lemon peel
2 cans (6 ounces each) crabmeat, drained
   and cartilage removed
¼ cup margarine or butter
2 cups half-and-half
¼ cup cracker crumbs
Salt and pepper
2 teaspoons sherry

Mix milk, mace and lemon peel in saucepan.
Simmer 2 to 3 minutes. Stir in crabmeat, margarine and half-and-half. Simmer 15 minutes.
Stir in cracker crumbs; season with salt and
pepper. Remove soup from heat; stir in sherry.

Shrimp Gumbo

2 medium onions, sliced
1 medium green pepper, cut into thin
  strips
2 cloves garlic, crushed
¼ cup margarine or butter
2 tablespoons all-purpose flour
3 cups water
1 tablespoon instant beef bouillon (dry)
1 teaspoon salt
¼ teaspoon pepper
½ teaspoon red pepper sauce
1 bay leaf
1 package (10 ounces) frozen cut okra,
  thawed
1 can (16 ounces) whole tomatoes,
  undrained
1 can (6 ounces) tomato paste
1½ pounds fresh or frozen raw shrimp
  (in shells*), thawed
3 cups hot cooked rice
¼ cup snipped parsley

Cook and stir onions, green pepper and garlic in margarine in Dutch oven over low heat until onions are tender. Stir in flour. Cook over low heat, stirring constantly, until bubbly; remove from heat. Stir in remaining ingredients except shrimp, rice and parsley; break up tomatoes with fork. Heat to boiling; reduce heat. Simmer uncovered, stirring occasionally, 45 minutes.

Peel shrimp. Make a shallow cut lengthwise down back of each shrimp; wash out sand vein. Stir shrimp into tomato mixture. Cover and simmer until shrimp are white, about 5 minutes. Remove bay leaf. Serve gumbo over rice; sprinkle with parsley.

*1 pound frozen peeled and deveined shrimp, thawed, can be substituted for the 1½ pounds shrimp in shells.

Following pages: Oriental Oyster Stew

· 3 ·

SOUFFLÉS AND OMELETS

Smoked Salmon and Broccoli Soufflé

4 SERVINGS

1 small onion, chopped
¼ cup margarine or butter
¼ cup all-purpose flour
⅛ teaspoon pepper
½ cup milk
½ cup chardonnay or dry white wine
3 eggs, separated
¼ teaspoon cream of tartar
1 package (10 ounces) frozen chopped broccoli, thawed and well drained
4 ounces smoked salmon, flaked or chopped

Heat oven to 350°. Grease 1-quart soufflé dish or casserole. Cook and stir onion in margarine in 2-quart saucepan over low heat until tender. Stir in flour and pepper. Cook over low heat, stirring constantly, until bubbly; remove from heat. Stir in milk until blended; stir in wine. Heat to boiling, stirring constantly. Boil and stir 1 minute; remove from heat.

Beat egg whites and cream of tartar in medium bowl on high speed until stiff but not dry. Beat egg yolks in small bowl on high speed until very thick and lemon colored, about 3 minutes; stir into wine mixture.

Stir about ¼ of the beaten egg whites into wine mixture. Fold wine mixture into remaining egg-white mixture. Gently fold in broccoli and salmon.

Carefully pour into soufflé dish. Bake uncovered until knife inserted halfway between center and edge comes out clean, 60 to 65 minutes. Gently divide soufflé into portions, using 2 forks. Serve immediately.

Scrambled Eggs with Smoked Salmon

4 SERVINGS

1 tablespoon margarine or butter
4 ounces smoked salmon, flaked or finely
  chopped
4 eggs
¼ cup water
¼ teaspoon pepper
1 tablespoon snipped dill
4 slices toast
Lemon slices
Dill

Heat margarine in 10-inch skillet over medium heat until hot and bubbly; cook salmon 1 minute. Beat eggs, water and pepper; pour into skillet. Cook uncovered over low heat, stirring occasionally, until eggs are thickened throughout but still moist, 3 to 5 minutes; sprinkle with snipped dill. Serve eggs on toast; garnish with lemon slices and dill.

Salmon Impossible Pie

6 SERVINGS

1 can (15½ ounces) salmon, drained
  and flaked
1 cup shredded Swiss cheese (4 ounces)
1 medium onion, chopped (about ½ cup)
2 tablespoons all-purpose flour
4 eggs
1 cup milk
¾ teaspoon salt
⅛ teaspoon red pepper sauce

Toss salmon, cheese, onion and flour. Spread in greased pie plate or quiche pan, 9 × 1¼ inches. Beat eggs slightly; beat in remaining ingredients. Pour egg mixture over salmon mixture. Bake uncovered in 350° oven until knife inserted in center comes out clean, 35 to 40 minutes. Let stand 10 minutes before cutting.

TUNA IMPOSSIBLE PIE: Substitute 2 cans (6½ ounces each) tuna in water, drained, for the canned salmon.

Smoked Fish Omelet

6 SERVINGS

6 eggs
1/2 cup milk
1 teaspoon flour
1/8 teaspoon pepper
2 tablespoons margarine or butter
2 tablespoons snipped fresh dill
3/4 pound smoked fish
1/4 cup sliced radishes

Beat eggs, milk, flour and pepper. Heat margarine in 10-inch skillet over medium heat until hot. Pour egg mixture into skillet; sprinkle with 1 tablespoon of the dill.

Cook until eggs are thickened throughout but still moist, 3 to 5 minutes. Gently lift edge with fork so that uncooked portion can flow to bottom. Arrange fish on eggs; place radishes in center of eggs. Sprinkle omelet with remaining dill. Cut into wedges to serve.

Stir-fried Shrimp with Eggs

4 SERVINGS

1/2 pound fresh or frozen raw shrimp
1 cup bean sprouts
3 tablespoons vegetable oil
1 teaspoon salt
6 eggs, slightly beaten
1/2 teaspoon salt
1/8 teaspoon white pepper
1/4 cup chopped green onions (with tops)
1/4 teaspoon sesame oil

Peel shrimp. (If shrimp is frozen, do not thaw; peel under running cold water.) Make a shallow cut lengthwise down back of each shrimp; wash out sand vein. Cut shrimp into 3/4-inch pieces. Rinse bean sprouts in cold water; drain.

Heat wok until 1 or 2 drops of water bubble and skitter when sprinkled in wok. Add vegetable oil; rotate wok to coat side. Add shrimp; stir-fry 1 minute. Add bean sprouts and 1 teaspoon salt; stir-fry 1 minute. Remove from wok to strainer.

Mix eggs, 1/2 teaspoon salt and the white pepper. Add shrimp, bean sprouts, eggs, green onions and sesame oil to wok; cook and stir until eggs are thickened throughout but are still moist.

Shrimp Egg Foo Yung

8 ounces bean sprouts
1 cup cooked shrimp
8 eggs, slightly beaten
1 jar (4½ ounces) sliced mushrooms,
   drained
2 green onions (with tops), chopped
½ teaspoon salt
3 tablespoons vegetable oil
1½ cups chicken broth
1 tablespoon dark soy sauce
1 teaspoon light soy sauce
¼ teaspoon salt
Dash of white pepper
2 tablespoons cornstarch
2 tablespoons cold water

Rinse bean sprouts in cold water; drain. Cut shrimp into ½-inch pieces. Stir bean sprouts, shrimp, eggs, mushrooms, green onions and ½ teaspoon salt just to blend.

Heat wok until 1 or 2 drops of water bubble and skitter when sprinkled in wok. Add vegetable oil; rotate wok to coat side. Reduce heat to medium-high. Pour ½ cup egg mixture into wok. Push cooked egg up over shrimp with broad spatula to form patty. Fry patty until set and golden brown, turning once, about 4 minutes. Repeat with remaining egg mixture. (Add vegetable oil if necessary.) Keep patties warm in 300° oven.

Heat chicken broth, the soy sauces, ¼ teaspoon salt and the white pepper to boiling. Mix cornstarch and water; stir into broth mixture. Cook and stir until thickened, about 10 seconds; pour over patties.

Do-ahead Tip: Fry egg patties; wrap, label and freeze no longer than 1 month. Just before serving, heat frozen patties uncovered in 375° oven until hot, about 25 minutes. Continue as directed.

Following pages: Shrimp Egg Foo Yung

Shrimp Soufflé

1/2 *pound raw shrimp**
1/4 *cup finely chopped onion*
1/4 *cup margarine or butter*
1/4 *cup all-purpose flour*
1/2 *teaspoon salt*
Dash of ground red pepper
1 cup milk
4 eggs, separated
1/4 *teaspoon cream of tartar*
Savory Sauce (page 39)

Peel shrimp. Make shallow cut lengthwise down back of each shrimp; wash out sand vein. Cut shrimp into 1/2-inch pieces. Cook and stir onion in margarine in 2-quart saucepan over medium heat until onion is tender, about 5 minutes. Add shrimp; cook and stir just until shrimp are pink, about 3 minutes. Remove shrimp with slotted spoon; reserve.

Blend flour, salt and ground red pepper into margarine. Cook over low heat, stirring constantly, until smooth and bubbly; remove from heat. Stir in milk. Heat to boiling, stirring constantly. Boil and stir 1 minute. Remove from heat; stir in shrimp.

Heat oven to 325°. Butter 6-cup soufflé dish or 1 1/2-quart casserole. Beat egg whites and cream of tartar in large bowl on high speed until stiff but not dry. Beat egg yolks in small bowl until very thick and lemon colored, about 5 minutes; stir into shrimp mixture. Stir about 1/4 of the egg whites into shrimp mixture. Fold shrimp mixture into remaining egg whites. Carefully pour into soufflé dish. Bake uncovered until knife inserted halfway between center and edge comes out clean, 50 to 60 minutes.

Prepare Savory Sauce. Gently divide soufflé into sections with 2 forks. Serve soufflé immediately with sauce.

SAVORY SAUCE

1 tablespoon margarine or butter
1 tablespoon all-purpose flour
1/2 teaspoon dried savory leaves
1/8 teaspoon pepper
3/4 cup milk
1/4 cup dry white wine

Heat margarine in 1-quart saucepan over low heat until melted. Blend in flour, savory and pepper. Cook over low heat, stirring constantly, until mixture is smooth and bubbly; remove from heat. Stir in milk. Heat to boiling, stirring constantly. Boil and stir 1 minute. Stir in wine; heat just to boiling.

*1 can (4 1/4 ounces) tiny shrimp, rinsed and drained, can be substituted for the cut-up cooked shrimp.

Herbed Crab Custards

4 SERVINGS

1/4 cup sliced green onions (with tops)
2 tablespoons margarine or butter
1 cup dairy sour cream
1/4 cup chenin blanc or dry white wine
1/4 cup milk
1 teaspoon snipped fresh tarragon leaves
   or 1/4 teaspoon dried tarragon leaves
1/2 teaspoon salt
4 eggs
1 package (6 ounces) frozen crabmeat,
   thawed and well drained, or 6 ounces
   imitation crabmeat, cut into 1/2-inch
   pieces

Heat oven to 350°. Cook and stir green onions in margarine in 1-quart saucepan over medium heat until tender; remove from heat.

Beat remaining ingredients except crabmeat until smooth; stir in onions and crabmeat. Pour mixture into 4 ungreased 10-ounce custard cups. Place cups in rectangular pan, 13 × 9 × 2 inches, on oven rack. Pour very hot water into pan to within 1/2 inch of tops of cups.

Bake until knife inserted halfway between center and edge comes out clean, 30 to 35 minutes. Serve immediately. Refrigerate any remaining custards.

Following pages: Herbed Crab Custards

Crab Scramble Casserole

1/4 cup margarine or butter, melted
12 eggs
1/2 cup milk
1 teaspoon salt
1/2 teaspoon white pepper
1 1/2 teaspoons snipped fresh dill or 1/2 teaspoon dried dill weed
1 can (6 ounces) crabmeat, drained and cartilage removed
1 package (8 ounces) cream cheese, cut into 1/2-inch cubes
Paprika

Pour margarine into square baking dish, 8 × 8 × 2 inches; tilt dish to coat bottom. Beat eggs, milk, salt, pepper and dill weed; stir in crabmeat and cheese. Pour into dish. Cover and refrigerate no longer than 24 hours.

Heat oven to 350°. Sprinkle egg mixture with paprika. Bake uncovered until center is set, 40 to 45 minutes.

Crabmeat Frittata

6 SERVINGS

4 ounces mushrooms, sliced, or 1 jar (4 ounces) sliced mushrooms, drained
1 bunch green onions (with tops), sliced
1/4 cup margarine or butter
1 package (6 ounces) frozen crabmeat, thawed and drained
8 eggs
1/2 teaspoon lemon and pepper seasoning salt
1 cup shredded Fontina or Monterey Jack cheese (4 ounces)
1 tablespoon snipped fresh basil leaves or 1 teaspoon dried basil leaves
2 tablespoons grated Parmesan cheese

Cook mushrooms and onions in margarine in 10-inch ovenproof skillet, stirring frequently, until tender, about 10 minutes. Stir in crabmeat.

Beat eggs and seasoning salt until blended; stir in Fontina cheese and basil. Pour over crabmeat mixture. Cover and cook over medium-low heat until eggs are set and light brown on bottom, 8 to 10 minutes.

Set oven control to broil. Broil frittata with top about 5 inches from heat until golden brown, about 2 minutes. Sprinkle with Parmesan cheese; cut into wedges.

· 4 ·

SALADS AND SANDWICHES

Marinated Shrimp Salad

4 cups water
1 tablespoon salt
1 pound raw shrimp, shelled and
  deveined
1 cup vegetable oil
1/3 cup lime juice
2 tablespoons snipped parsley
1/2 teaspoon salt
4 green onions (with tops), thinly sliced
2 tomatoes, seeded and chopped
2 cloves garlic, chopped
8 to 10 drops aromatic bitters
Dash of crushed red pepper
1 avocado, peeled and chopped
Lettuce leaves
Lime wedges

Heat water to boiling in 3-quart saucepan. Add 1 tablespoon salt and the shrimp. Cover and heat to boiling; reduce heat. Simmer until shrimp are pink, about 3 minutes; drain.

Mix oil, lime juice, parsley, 1/2 teaspoon salt, the green onions, tomatoes, garlic, bitters and red pepper in large bowl; stir in shrimp. Cover and refrigerate at least 6 hours. Just before serving, carefully stir in avocado. Spoon shrimp mixture onto lettuce-lined plates with slotted spoon. Garnish with lime wedges. Serve remaining marinade with salads, if desired.

Greek Seafood Salad

¾ *cup water*
1 *tablespoon margarine or butter*
¼ *teaspoon salt*
½ *cup uncooked couscous**
2 *tablespoons snipped parsley*
½ *medium cucumber, chopped*
4 *medium radishes, chopped*
1 *package (6 ounces) frozen cooked*
  shrimp, thawed, or 1½ cups cut-up
  cooked crabmeat
3 *tablespoons olive or vegetable oil*
2 *tablespoons lemon juice*
1 *teaspoon salt*
⅛ *teaspoon pepper*
½ *cup whipping cream*
1 *teaspoon Dijon-style mustard*
6 *large tomatoes*

Heat water, margarine and ¼ teaspoon salt to boiling in 1-quart saucepan; add couscous. Cover and remove from heat; let stand 5 minutes. Mix couscous, parsley, cucumber, radishes and shrimp in large bowl. Sprinkle with oil, lemon juice, 1 teaspoon salt and the pepper; stir until evenly coated. Cover and refrigerate until chilled, about 2 hours.

Beat whipping cream and mustard in chilled bowl until soft peaks form; stir into couscous mixture. Cut stem ends from tomatoes. Place tomatoes, cut sides down on plate; cut each into sixths to within ½ inch of bottom. Carefully spread out sections. Fill with couscous mixture. Serve on lettuce leaves and garnish with additional parsley, if desired.

*1½ cups cooked rice can be substituted for the cooked couscous.

Crab Louis

4 *cups bite-size pieces salad greens*
2 *cups cut-up cooked crabmeat or 1 pack-*
  age (8 ounces) frozen salad-style im-
  itation crabmeat, thawed
4 *tomatoes, cut into fourths*
4 *hard-cooked eggs, cut into fourths*
Ripe or pimiento-stuffed olives
Louis Dressing (page 45)

Divide salad greens among 4 large individual salad bowls or plates. Arrange crabmeat, tomatoes, eggs and olives on lettuce. Pour Louis Dressing over salads.

LOUIS DRESSING

¾ cup chili sauce
½ cup mayonnaise or salad dressing
1 teaspoon finely chopped onion
½ teaspoon sugar
¼ teaspoon Worcestershire sauce
Salt to taste

Mix all ingredients; refrigerate 30 minutes.

Chilled Shrimp, Pea Pods and Bean Curd   6 SERVINGS

8 ounces bean curd
8 ounces fresh or frozen raw shrimp
4 cups water
1 tablespoon salt
1 package (6 ounces) frozen Chinese pea
  pods
1 green onion, finely chopped
2 tablespoons soy sauce
1 tablespoon sesame oil

Cut bean curd into 3 slices; carefully place in sieve. Blanch bean curd in boiling water 30 seconds; drain. Cut each slice into 3 strips; cut each strip diagonally into 1-inch pieces.

Peel shrimp. (If shrimp are frozen, do not thaw; peel under running cold water.) Make a shallow cut lengthwise down back of each shrimp; wash out sand vein. Heat water to boiling. Add shrimp and salt. Cover and heat to boiling; reduce heat. Simmer until shrimp are pink, about 5 minutes; drain.

Cook pea pods as directed on package; drain. Place bean curd, shrimp, pea pods and green onion in bowl. Mix soy sauce and sesame oil; pour over shrimp mixture. Toss lightly. Cover and refrigerate at least 1 hour.

Seafood Salad with Dill Dressing

Creamy Dill Dressing (below)
1½ cups cooked medium shrimp (about ½ pound shelled)*
1 cup cut-up cooked crabmeat**
¼ cup sliced green onions (with tops)
1 medium cucumber, chopped
1 can (8½ ounces) sliced water chestnuts, drained
2 avocados, peeled and sliced
Salad greens

Prepare Creamy Dill Dressing; toss with remaining ingredients except avocados and salad greens. Cover and refrigerate at least 1 hour.

Arrange avocados on salad greens. Top with shrimp mixture.

CREAMY DILL DRESSING

½ cup mayonnaise or salad dressing
¼ cup dairy sour cream or plain yogurt
2 tablespoons lemon juice
1 teaspoon snipped fresh dill or ¼ teaspoon dried dill weed
¼ teaspoon salt

Mix all ingredients.

*1 package (6 ounces) frozen cooked medium shrimp, thawed, or 2 cans (4½ ounces each) large shrimp, drained, can be substituted for the fresh shrimp.

**1 package (6 ounces) frozen cooked crabmeat, thawed, drained and cartilage removed, can be substituted for the fresh crabmeat.

Seafood–Wild Rice Salad

½ cup mayonnaise or salad dressing
1 tablespoon lemon juice
1 teaspoon curry powder
2 cups cold cooked wild rice
½ cup frozen green peas, thawed
2 tablespoons chopped pimiento
2 packages (6 ounces each) frozen crab-
*   meat, thawed, drained and cartilage*
*   removed*
2 cans (4¼ ounces each) medium shrimp,
*   rinsed and drained*
Salad greens
Cherry tomatoes or tomato wedges

Mix mayonnaise, lemon juice and curry powder in 2½-quart bowl. Add wild rice, peas, pimiento, crabmeat and shrimp; toss. Cover and refrigerate at least 1 hour.

Spoon onto salad greens; garnish with cherry tomatoes.

Warm Scallop Salad

1 pound fresh scallops or frozen scal-
*   lops, thawed*
4 ounces mushrooms, sliced (about
*   1½ cups)*
1 small leek (with green top), sliced (about
*   ⅓ cup)*
2 tablespoons margarine or butter
2 tablespoons olive or vegetable oil
½ cup sémillon or dry white wine
½ teaspoon snipped fresh tarragon leaves
*   or ⅛ teaspoon dried tarragon leaves*
2 tablespoons cold water
2 teaspoons cornstarch
3 cups shredded assorted greens
1 lemon, cut into wedges

If scallops are large, cut into 1-inch pieces. Cook and stir mushrooms and leek in margarine and oil in 10-inch skillet 5 minutes. Stir in wine and tarragon. Heat to boiling. Add scallops; reduce heat. Simmer uncovered, stirring occasionally, until scallops turn white, 3 to 4 minutes. Mix water and cornstarch; stir into scallop mixture. Heat to boiling. Boil and stir 1 minute. Spoon scallop mixture over greens; garnish with lemon wedges.

Following pages: Seafood–Wild Rice Salad

Grilled Salmon Salad

4 small salmon steaks, each about
   1 inch thick (about 1½ pounds)
1 tablespoon snipped fresh marjoram
   leaves or 1 teaspoon dried marjoram leaves
½ teaspoon salt
¼ teaspoon pepper
½ cup oil-and-vinegar dressing
6 cups mixed salad greens
2 tablespoons capers, drained

Sprinkle salmon steaks with marjoram, salt and pepper. Set oven control to broil. Place salmon on rack in broiler pan; drizzle with 1 tablespoon of the dressing.

Broil salmon with tops about 3 inches from heat until opaque, 7 to 10 minutes. Turn; drizzle with 1 tablespoon dressing. Broil until salmon flakes easily with fork, about 5 minutes longer.

Mix salad greens and capers; toss with remaining dressing. Divide among 4 plates; top with salmon steaks.

Salmon and Grapefruit Salad

1 container (6 ounces) plain yogurt
1 tablespoon grated grapefruit peel
3 cups bite-size pieces salad greens
1 tablespoon tarragon vinegar
1 teaspoon seasoned salt
2 stalks celery, cut into thin diagonal
   slices
1 grapefruit, pared and sectioned
1 can (15½ ounces) salmon, drained and
   flaked

Mix yogurt and grapefruit peel; cover and refrigerate. Just before serving, toss remaining ingredients. Serve with yogurt dressing and, if desired, on salad greens.

Salmon-Squash Salads

Sesame Dressing (below)
*1 small zucchini, thinly sliced (about
    1½ cups)*
*1 small yellow summer squash, thinly
    sliced (about 1½ cups)*
*2 medium stalks celery, sliced (about
    1 cup)*
*1 small onion, sliced and separated into
    rings*
1 cup sliced mushrooms
Lettuce cups or leaves
*1 can (15½ ounces) salmon, chilled,
    drained and flaked*
12 cherry tomatoes

Prepare Sesame Dressing. Toss zucchini, summer squash, celery, onion and mushrooms. Spoon into lettuce cups on each of 6 plates. Place salmon chunks on center of vegetable mixture; top with 2 cherry tomatoes. Spoon Sesame Dressing over salads.

SESAME DRESSING

1 tablespoon sesame seed
⅓ cup white wine vinegar
1 tablespoon sugar
2 tablespoons vegetable oil
1 teaspoon dry mustard
½ teaspoon salt
1 large clove garlic, crushed

Cook and stir sesame seed over medium heat until golden brown; cool. Shake seed and remaining ingredients in tightly covered container. Refrigerate until chilled, about 2 hours. Remove garlic and shake before serving.

TUNA-SQUASH SALADS: Substitute 2 cans (6½ ounces each) tuna in water, chilled and drained, for the salmon.

Herring Salad

1 jar (22 ounces) herring cutlets in wine
  sauce, drained
3 medium potatoes, cooked and cubed
  (2 cups)
1 jar (16 ounces) pickled beets, drained
  and cubed
2 small dill pickles, chopped
1 apple, cut up
1 small onion, chopped
1/4 cup vinegar
2 tablespoons sugar
2 tablespoons water
1/8 teaspoon pepper
Dilled Sour Cream (below)

Place herring, potatoes, beets, pickles, apple and onion in glass or plastic bowl. Mix vinegar, sugar, water and pepper; pour over herring mixture. Toss lightly. Cover and refrigerate, stirring once or twice, at least 2 hours. Serve with Dilled Sour Cream. Garnish with parsley and wedges of hard-cooked egg, if desired.

DILLED SOUR CREAM

1 cup dairy sour cream
2 tablespoons milk
1 1/2 teaspoons snipped fresh dill or 1/2 teaspoon dried dill weed

Mix all ingredients.

Layered Tuna Salad

1 pared or unpared tart eating apple,
  cut into cubes
2 tablespoons lemon juice
3 cups bite-size pieces spinach (about
  6 ounces)
1 can (9¼ ounces) tuna, drained
4 ounces bean sprouts
1 can (8 ounces) sliced water chestnuts,
  drained
1 cup mayonnaise or salad dressing
2 tablespoons grated Parmesan cheese
1 tablespoon Chinese-style or Dijon-style
  mustard
1 teaspoon Worcestershire sauce
2 green onions (with tops), thinly sliced

Toss apple cubes and lemon juice. Place about half of the spinach in large glass bowl. Layer with tuna, apple, bean sprouts, remaining spinach and water chestnuts.

Mix remaining ingredients except onions; spread over water chestnuts, sealing to edge of bowl. Sprinkle with onions. Cover and refrigerate at least 2 hours but no longer than 24 hours.

Tuna and Tomato Salad

¼ cup olive or vegetable oil
¼ cup wine vinegar
½ teaspoon red pepper sauce
2 medium tomatoes, coarsely chopped
1 bunch green onions (with tops), sliced
1 clove garlic, crushed
1 can (9¼ ounces) tuna, drained
½ pound fresh asparagus, cut diagonally
  into 1-inch pieces*
6 cups bite-size pieces salad greens
Freshly ground pepper

Mix oil, vinegar, pepper sauce, tomatoes, onions, garlic and tuna in 4-quart bowl. Layer asparagus and salad greens on tuna mixture. Cover and refrigerate at least 2 hours but no longer than 24 hours. Sprinkle with pepper and toss just before serving.

*2 cups chopped broccoli can be substituted for the asparagus.

Curried Egg and Shrimp Sandwiches

6 OPEN-FACE SANDWICHES

1 package (8 ounces) cream cheese,
  softened
1/4 cup dairy sour cream
1 teaspoon curry powder
1/4 teaspoon salt
6 slices multigrain bread, toasted
3 hard-cooked eggs, sliced
1 can (4¼ ounces) tiny shrimp, drained
1/4 cup finely chopped green onions (with
  tops)

Mix cream cheese, sour cream, curry powder and salt; spread over toast. Arrange egg slices on cream cheese mixture. Top with shrimp and onions.

Shrimp and Avocado Club Sandwiches

4 SANDWICHES

Mayonnaise or salad dressing
12 slices white bread, toasted
4 lettuce leaves
12 slices tomatoes (about 2 medium)
12 slices bacon, crisply cooked
2 cans (4¼ ounces each) large shrimp,
  rinsed and drained
1 large avocado, peeled and thinly sliced

Spread mayonnaise over one side of each slice toast. Place lettuce leaf, 3 slices tomato and 3 slices bacon on each of 4 slices toast. Top with another slice toast.

Arrange shrimp on top; arrange avocado slices on shrimp. Top with third slice toast; secure with wooden picks. Cut sandwiches diagonally into 4 triangles.

Seafood Salad in Pita

8 SANDWICHES

1/2 cup mayonnaise or salad dressing
1 tablespoon finely chopped green onion
(with top)
1/2 teaspoon salt
Dash of pepper
2 cups cut-up cooked shrimp or
crabmeat or 1 package (8 ounces) fro-
zen salad-style imitation crabmeat,
thawed*
2 cups thinly sliced celery
4 pita breads (6-inch)
Tomato slices
Alfalfa sprouts

Mix mayonnaise, onion, salt and pepper; toss with shrimp and celery. Cover tightly and refrigerate at least 2 hours. Cut pita breads crosswise into halves. Fill each half with about 1/2 cup shrimp mixture. Insert tomato slices and alfalfa sprouts in each.

LOBSTER ROLLS: Substitute cut-up cooked lobster for the shrimp and 8 hot dog buns, toasted, for the pita breads. Omit tomatoes and alfalfa sprouts.

*Two packages (6 ounces each) frozen cooked crabmeat, thawed, or 2 cans (6 ounces each) crabmeat, drained and cartilage removed, can be substituted for the fresh or imitation crabmeat.

Broiled Seafood Sandwiches

4 OPEN-FACE SANDWICHES

1 cup mixed bite-size pieces cooked
crabmeat, lobster or shrimp*
1 cup shredded Swiss cheese (4 ounces)
1/2 cup mayonnaise or salad dressing
1 green onion (with top), thinly sliced
4 slices whole grain bread, toasted
Alfalfa sprouts

Mix all ingredients except toast and sprouts. Set oven control to broil. Arrange sprouts on toast; top with seafood mixture.

Place sandwiches on ungreased cookie sheet. Broil with tops about 4 inches from heat until seafood mixture is hot and bubbly, about 2 minutes.

*1 cup bite-size pieces cooked fish (salmon, cod, halibut, tuna, swordfish) can be substituted for the crabmeat, lobster or shrimp.

Following pages: Curried Egg and Shrimp Sandwiches

Tunawiches

6 OPEN-FACE SANDWICHES

½ loaf (1-pound size) French bread
Spicy brown mustard
½ cup mayonnaise or salad dressing
2 cans (6½ ounces each) tuna, drained
1 cup shredded Muenster cheese
   (4 ounces)
Salad greens
1 medium cucumber, thinly sliced
1 medium tomato, cut into 6 slices

Cut loaf of bread lengthwise into halves; spread mustard over cut sides. Mix mayonnaise and tuna; spread on mustard.

Top with cheese, salad greens, cucumber and tomato. Cut each bread half into thirds. Spoon dollop of mayonnaise onto each sandwich, if desired.

Tuna Cobb Salad Sandwiches

4 SANDWICHES

1 can (6½ ounces) tuna, drained
4 to 6 slices bacon, crisply cooked and
   crumbled
2 hard-cooked eggs, chopped
1 avocado, peeled and cut into cubes
¼ to ⅓ cup blue cheese dressing
Shredded iceberg lettuce or romaine
2 medium tomatoes, thinly sliced
4 croissants, split

Mix tuna, bacon, eggs, avocado and dressing. Place lettuce and tomatoes on bottom halves of croissants. Spoon tuna mixture on tomatoes; top with remaining halves.

Tuna Patty Sandwiches

1 egg, slightly beaten
1 can (9¹/₄ ounces) tuna, drained
4 green onions (with tops), chopped
¹/₄ cup cracker crumbs
1 tablespoon lemon juice
¹/₂ teaspoon salt
¹/₄ teaspoon pepper
2 tablespoons margarine or butter
4 hamburger buns, split and toasted
4 slices process American cheese
Lettuce leaves
1 tomato, sliced
¹/₄ cup Tartar Sauce (page 106)

Mix egg, tuna, onions, cracker crumbs, lemon juice, salt and pepper. Shape into 4 patties, each about ¹/₂ inch thick. Heat margarine in 10-inch skillet over medium heat until melted. Cook patties in margarine until golden brown, about 5 minutes on each side.

Place a patty on each of 4 bun halves. Top each with cheese slice, lettuce, tomato, Tartar Sauce and remaining bun half.

SALMON PATTY SANDWICHES: Substitute 1 can (15¹/₂ ounces) salmon, drained and flaked, for the tuna.

·5·

FIN FISH

Sole with Red Grapes

1½ pounds sole fillets
1¼ cups water
⅓ cup dry white wine
1 tablespoon lemon juice
½ teaspoon salt
¼ teaspoon pepper
3 green onions (with tops), sliced
½ cup whipping cream
2 tablespoons all-purpose flour
1 cup seedless red or green grapes

If fish fillets are large, cut into 6 serving pieces. Place fish in 10-inch skillet; add water, wine, lemon juice, salt, pepper and onions. Heat to boiling; reduce heat. Cover and simmer until fish flakes easily with fork, 5 to 6 minutes. Remove fish with slotted spatula; keep warm.

Shake whipping cream and flour in tightly covered container; stir into liquid in skillet. Heat to boiling. Continue boiling, stirring frequently, until slightly thickened, about 10 minutes. Add grapes; heat until hot. Spoon sauce over fish.

Southern-fried Catfish

Vegetable oil
1¼ cups cornmeal
1 teaspoon salt
½ teaspoon ground red pepper
¼ teaspoon pepper
6 small catfish (about ½ pound each),
  skinned and pan-dressed (page 97)
½ cup all-purpose flour
2 eggs, slightly beaten

Heat oil (½ inch) in 12-inch skillet over medium-high heat until hot. Mix cornmeal, salt, red pepper and pepper; reserve. Coat catfish with flour; dip into eggs. Coat with cornmeal mixture. Fry catfish, 2 at a time, until golden brown, about 6 minutes on each side. Keep warm in 275° oven while frying remaining catfish.

Orange Almond Trout

1 pound trout fillets
¼ cup sliced almonds
1 medium onion, sliced
¼ cup margarine or butter
½ cup all-purpose flour
½ teaspoon salt
½ teaspoon paprika
⅛ teaspoon pepper
2 oranges, pared and sectioned

If fish fillets are large, cut into 5 serving pieces. Cook and stir almonds and onion in margarine in 10-inch skillet until onion is tender; remove with slotted spoon and keep warm. Mix flour, salt, paprika and pepper. Coat fish with flour mixture. Cook fish in same skillet over medium heat, turning carefully, until brown, about 10 minutes. Top with almonds and onion; garnish with orange sections.

Following pages: Sole with Red Grapes

Trout with Cabbage and Apples

4 SERVINGS

5 cups coarsely shredded cabbage (about
    ½ large head)
¾ cup gewürztraminer or dry white wine
¼ teaspoon salt
¼ teaspoon caraway seed
2 green onions (with tops), thinly sliced
2 medium unpared tart cooking apples,
    coarsely chopped
4 pan-dressed rainbow trout or white-
    fish (8 to 10 ounces each)
Vegetable oil

Heat oven to 400°. Heat cabbage, wine, salt, caraway seed and green onions to boiling in 3-quart saucepan; reduce heat. Simmer uncovered, stirring frequently, just until cabbage is limp, about 1 minute. Stir in apples.

Place mixture in ungreased rectangular baking dish, 13 × 9 × 2 inches. Arrange fish on top; brush fish with oil. Bake uncovered until fish flakes easily with fork, about 25 minutes. Garnish with apple slices, if desired.

Pompano en Papillote

4 SERVINGS

2 cups water
½ cup dry white wine
½ teaspoon salt
1 medium onion, sliced
3 slices lemon
3 sprigs parsley
1 bay leaf
4 peppercorns
1 pound pompano fillets, cut into 4 equal
    pieces*
Mushroom Sauce (page 65)
4 pieces kitchen parchment paper or alu-
    minum foil, 12 × 15 inches
Vegetable oil
12 cleaned medium raw shrimp (about
    1 cup)

Heat water, wine, salt, onion, lemon, parsley, bay leaf and peppercorns to boiling in 12-inch skillet; reduce heat. Cover and simmer 5 minutes. Place pompano fillets in skillet. Heat to boiling; reduce heat. Simmer uncovered until fish flakes easily with fork, 3 to 6 minutes. Carefully remove fish with slotted spoon; drain on wire rack. Reserve cooking liquid in skillet.

Heat oven to 400°. Prepare Mushroom Sauce. Cut each piece of parchment paper into heart shape, about 12 inches long by 14 inches wide. Brush oil on top of each heart to within ½ inch of edge.

Spoon ¼ cup Mushroom Sauce onto half of each heart. Place 1 piece of fish on sauce. Arrange 3 shrimp on fish; spoon about 1 tablespoon sauce over shrimp. Fold other half of heart over top. Beginning at top of heart, seal edges by turning up and folding together; twist tip of heart to hold packet closed. Bake on ungreased cookie sheet until paper puffs up and is light brown, about 15 minutes. To serve, cut a large X shape on top of each packet; fold back corners.

MUSHROOM SAUCE

Reserved cooking liquid
1 cup sliced mushrooms
3 tablespoons margarine or butter
3 tablespoons all-purpose flour
¼ teaspoon salt
⅛ teaspoon white pepper
¼ cup half-and-half

Strain reserved cooking liquid. Heat to boiling; continue boiling until liquid measures 1 cup. Cook mushrooms and margarine in 1½-quart saucepan over low heat, stirring occasionally, until mushrooms are tender, about 5 minutes. Stir in flour, salt and pepper. Cook over low heat, stirring constantly, until smooth and bubbly; remove from heat. Gradually stir in liquid and half-and-half. Heat to boiling, stirring constantly. Boil and stir 1 minute.

*Trout, pike, halibut, haddock or orange roughy fillets can be substituted for the pompano fillets.

Following pages: Pompano en Papillote

Ginger-sauced Fish

2-pound pan-dressed pike or sea bass
2 tablespoons lemon juice
1 tablespoon vegetable oil
2 teaspoons finely chopped gingerroot
1/2 teaspoon salt
2 green onions (with tops)
Ginger Sauce (below)

Remove head from fish. Slash fish crosswise 3 times on each side. Mix lemon juice, oil, gingerroot and salt; brush in cavity and on outside of fish. Cover and refrigerate 1 hour.

Place fish on rack over water in steamer or roasting pan (water should not touch rack; if necessary, elevate rack by placing on custard cups). Cover tightly and heat to boiling; reduce heat. Steam over simmering water until fish flakes easily with fork, about 20 minutes. (Add more boiling water if necessary.)

Cut green onions into 2-inch pieces; cut pieces into thin strips. Prepare Ginger Sauce. Carefully remove skin from hot fish and discard; place fish on warm platter. Pour half of the Ginger Sauce over fish; sprinkle with green onions. Serve with remaining Ginger Sauce.

GINGER SAUCE

1 tablespoon finely chopped gingerroot
1 teaspoon finely chopped garlic
2 tablespoons vegetable oil
1/2 cup Pinot blanc or dry white wine
1/4 cup soy sauce
1/4 cup chili sauce
1/2 teaspoon sugar
4 to 6 drops red pepper sauce
1 tablespoon cornstarch
2 tablespoons cold water

Cook and stir gingerroot and garlic in oil in 1-quart saucepan until light brown. Stir in remaining ingredients except cornstarch and water. Heat to boiling; reduce heat. Cover and simmer 10 minutes. Mix cornstarch and cold water; stir into ginger mixture. Heat to boiling; boil and stir 1 minute.

Sea Bass in Cilantro

2 pounds sea bass or red snapper fillets, cut into 8 serving pieces
1 cup milk
1 teaspoon ground cumin
1 large onion, finely chopped (about
  1 cup)
1/4 cup vegetable oil
1 cup finely chopped canned green chilies
1/4 to 1/2 cup snipped fresh cilantro
3/4 teaspoon salt
1/4 teaspoon pepper
Lime or lemon wedges

Place fish fillets in shallow glass or plastic dish. Mix milk and cumin; pour over fish. Cover and refrigerate 1 hour.

Cook and stir onion in oil in 2-quart saucepan until tender. Stir in remaining ingredients except fish and lime wedges. Heat to boiling; reduce heat. Simmer uncovered until thickened, about 10 minutes.

Heat oven to 350°. Drain fish; pat dry. Place 1 piece fish on each of eight 12-inch squares heavy-duty aluminum foil. Spoon some onion mixture onto fish. Fold foil over fish; seal securely. Place foil packets in ungreased jelly roll pan, 15½ × 10½ × 1 inch. Bake until fish flakes easily with fork, 25 to 30 minutes. Serve with lime wedges.

Baked Red Snapper

2 pounds red snapper fillets, cut into
  8 serving pieces
1 cup milk
1 tablespoon snipped fresh oregano leaves
1 medium onion, sliced
1/4 cup olive or vegetable oil
1/2 cup pitted ripe olives
1/4 cup dry white wine
1/4 cup lemon juice
2 tablespoons capers
1 teaspoon ground cumin
1/2 teaspoon salt
1/4 teaspoon pepper
4 large tomatoes, chopped (about 4 cups)
2 cloves garlic, finely chopped

Place fish fillets in shallow glass or plastic dish. Mix milk and oregano; pour over fish. Cover and refrigerate 1 hour.

Cook and stir onion in oil in 10-inch skillet until tender. Stir in remaining ingredients except fish. Simmer uncovered until thickened, about 15 minutes.

Heat oven to 350°. Drain fish; pat dry. Place 1 piece fish on each of eight 12-inch squares heavy-duty aluminum foil. Spoon some tomato mixture onto fish. Fold foil over fish; seal securely. Place foil packets in ungreased jelly roll pan, 15½ × 10½ × 1 inch. Bake until fish flakes easily with fork, about 30 minutes.

Salmon with Creamy Cucumber Salsa

Creamy Cucumber Salsa (below)
2 cups water
1 cup dry white wine
1 teaspoon salt
¾ teaspoon snipped fresh thyme leaves
  or ¼ teaspoon dried thyme leaves
¾ teaspoon snipped fresh oregano leaves
  or ¼ teaspoon dried oregano leaves
⅛ teaspoon ground red pepper
4 black peppercorns
4 cilantro sprigs
1 small onion, sliced
2 pounds salmon fillets, cut into 6 serv-
  ing pieces

Prepare Creamy Cucumber Salsa; reserve. Heat remaining ingredients except fish fillets to boiling in 12-inch skillet; reduce heat. Cover and simmer 5 minutes.

Place fish in skillet; if necessary, add water so that fish is covered. Heat to boiling; reduce heat. Simmer uncovered until fish flakes easily with fork, about 14 minutes.

Carefully remove fish from skillet with slotted spatula; drain on wire rack. Cover and refrigerate until cold, about 2 hours. Serve with Creamy Cucumber Salsa.

CREAMY CUCUMBER SALSA

1 cup dairy sour cream
1 cup plain yogurt
¼ cup snipped parsley
¼ cup snipped fresh cilantro
1 teaspoon ground cumin
½ teaspoon salt
2 medium cucumbers, pared, seeded and
  coarsely shredded

Mix all ingredients. Cover and refrigerate until chilled, about 2 hours.

Baked Salmon Steaks

2 tablespoons lemon juice
1/4 cup packed brown sugar
4 salmon steaks, 1 inch thick (about
   2 pounds)
1 tablespoon margarine or butter, melted
4 thin slices lemon
8 teaspoons brown sugar

Heat oven to 375°. Pour lemon juice into ungreased rectangular baking dish, 11 × 7½ × 2 inches; sprinkle with ¼ cup brown sugar. Arrange salmon steaks in dish; drizzle with margarine. Bake uncovered 15 minutes; turn. Place 1 slice lemon on each salmon steak; sprinkle with 2 teaspoons brown sugar. Bake until fish flakes easily with fork, 15 to 20 minutes longer. Serve with juices from dish.

Baked Halibut with Cilantro Pesto

Cilantro Pesto (below)
6 halibut steaks, 1 inch thick (about
   5 ounces each)
2 tablespoons margarine or butter, melted
2 tablespoons lemon juice

Prepare Cilantro Pesto; reserve. Heat oven to 450°. Place fish steaks in ungreased rectangular baking dish, 13 × 9 × 2 inches. Mix margarine and lemon juice; pour over fish.

Bake uncovered until fish flakes easily with fork, 20 to 25 minutes. Serve with reserved Cilantro Pesto.

CILANTRO PESTO

1½ cups firmly packed fresh cilantro
½ cup firmly packed fresh parsley
½ cup grated Parmesan cheese
½ cup vegetable oil
¼ teaspoon salt
3 cloves garlic
¼ cup pine nuts (1 ounce)

Place all ingredients in food processor workbowl fitted with steel blade or in blender container; cover and process until well blended.

Following pages: Baked Halibut with Cilantro Pesto

Cod and Vegetable Bake

6 SERVINGS

2 pounds cod fillets
3 tablespoons lemon juice
1½ teaspoons salt
⅛ teaspoon pepper
½ cup margarine or butter, melted
½ teaspoon salt
½ teaspoon ground sage
½ teaspoon ground thyme
5 slices bread (crusts removed), cut into
     cubes
2 medium carrots, coarsely shredded
1 large stalk celery, finely chopped
1 medium onion, chopped (about ½ cup)
3 tablespoons dry bread crumbs
2 tablespoons snipped parsley
½ teaspoon paprika

If cod fillets are large, cut into 6 serving pieces. Arrange fish in ungreased rectangular baking dish, 12 × 7½ × 2 inches, or square baking dish, 8 × 8 × 2 inches. Sprinkle with lemon juice, 1½ teaspoons salt and the pepper.

Mix margarine, ½ teaspoon salt, sage, thyme, bread cubes, carrots, celery and onion. Spread evenly over fish. Mix bread crumbs, parsley and paprika; sprinkle over vegetables. Cover and bake in 350° oven until fish flakes easily with fork, about 35 minutes.

Wild Rice-stuffed Red Snapper

6 SERVINGS

Wild Rice Stuffing (page 75)
2½- to 3-pound red snapper, whitefish
     or northern pike, cleaned
Lemon juice
Salt
Vegetable oil
¼ cup margarine or butter, melted
2 tablespoons lemon juice
Lemon wedges

Prepare Wild Rice Stuffing. Rub cavity of snapper with lemon juice; sprinkle with salt. Loosely stuff with Wild Rice Stuffing. Close opening with skewers and lace with string. (Spoon any remaining stuffing into buttered baking dish; cover and refrigerate. Place in oven with snapper 30 minutes before snapper is done.)

Brush snapper with oil; place in shallow roasting pan. Mix margarine and 2 tablespoons lemon juice. Bake snapper uncovered in 350° oven, brushing occasionally with margarine mixture, until snapper flakes easily with fork, 50 to 60 minutes. Serve with lemon wedges.

WILD RICE STUFFING

¾ *cup uncooked wild rice*
2 *cups water*
1½ *teaspoons instant chicken bouillon*
½ *cup thinly sliced celery*
½ *cup chopped onion*
¼ *cup slivered almonds*
¼ *cup margarine or butter*
8 *ounces mushrooms, sliced (about*
   2½ cups)

Heat rice, water and bouillon (dry) to boiling, stirring once or twice; reduce heat. Cover and simmer until tender, 40 to 50 minutes. After cooking rice 30 minutes, check to see that rice is not sticking to pan. Add 2 to 3 tablespoons water if necessary.

Cook and stir celery, onion and almonds in margarine in 10-inch skillet over medium heat until vegetables are tender and almonds are light brown. Add mushrooms; cook until tender, about 5 minutes longer. Stir in wild rice.

Steamed Fish

2 SERVINGS

1½ *pounds walleye or sea bass, drawn*
1 *teaspoon finely chopped gingerroot*
2 *tablespoons vegetable oil*
2 *tablespoons brown bean sauce*
2 *cloves garlic, finely chopped*
1 *teaspoon salt*
1 *teaspoon soy sauce (light or dark)*
¼ *teaspoon sesame oil*
2 *green onions (with tops)*

Slash fish crosswise 3 times on each side. Mix gingerroot, vegetable oil, bean sauce, garlic, salt, soy sauce and sesame oil; rub cavity and outside of fish with mixture. Cover and refrigerate 40 minutes.

Cut green onions into 2-inch pieces; cut pieces lengthwise into thin strips. Place fish on heatproof plate. Place plate on rack in steamer; cover and steam over boiling water until fish flakes easily with fork, about 15 minutes. (Add boiling water if necessary.) Garnish with green onion strips.

Following pages: Wild Rice-stuffed Red Snapper

Stir-fried Fish with Pea Pods

4 SERVINGS

1 pound walleye or sea bass fillets
1 tablespoon vegetable oil
1 teaspoon cornstarch
1 teaspoon salt
1 teaspoon light soy sauce
1/4 teaspoon sesame oil
1/8 teaspoon white pepper
8 ounces pea pods
3 green onions (with tops)
3 tablespoons vegetable oil
1 clove garlic, finely chopped
1 teaspoon finely chopped gingerroot
2 tablespoons oyster sauce

Cut fish into strips, 2 × 1 inch. Toss fish strips, 1 tablespoon vegetable oil, the cornstarch, salt, soy sauce, sesame oil and white pepper in glass or plastic bowl. Cover and refrigerate 30 minutes. Remove strings from pea pods. Place pea pods in boiling water. Cover and cook 1 minute; drain. Immediately rinse under running cold water; drain. Cut green onions into 2-inch pieces.

Heat wok until 1 or 2 drops of water bubble and skitter when sprinkled in wok. Add 3 tablespoons vegetable oil; rotate wok to coat side. Add fish mixture, garlic and gingerroot; stir-fry until fish turns white. Add pea pods and green onions; stir-fry 1 minute. Stir in oyster sauce.

Baked Fish with Grapefruit Sauce

8 SERVINGS

2 to 2 1/2 pounds whole fish (whitefish, pike, salmon, lake trout or bass)
1 teaspoon salt
1/4 teaspoon snipped fresh dill or 1/8 teaspoon dried dill weed
1 small onion, sliced
1 lemon, sliced
1/4 cup margarine or butter, melted
2 tablespoons lemon juice
Grapefruit Sauce (page 79)

Remove head from fish. Rub cavity of fish with salt and sprinkle with dill weed. Place onion and lemon in cavity. Place fish in greased jelly roll pan, 15 1/2 × 10 1/2 × 1 inch. Mix margarine and lemon juice; brush fish with margarine mixture. Cook uncovered in 350° oven, brushing occasionally with margarine mixture, until fish flakes easily with fork, about 1 hour. Prepare Grapefruit Sauce; serve over fish. Garnish with fresh dill or parsley, if desired.

GRAPEFRUIT SAUCE

½ *cup unsweetened pink grapefruit juice*
⅛ *teaspoon salt*
Dash of dried dill weed
1 *teaspoon cornstarch*
1 *tablespoon cold water*
1 *pink grapefruit, pared and sectioned*

Heat grapefruit juice, salt and dill weed to boiling in 1½-quart saucepan. Mix cornstarch and cold water; stir into grapefruit juice. Heat to boiling; boil and stir 1 minute. Carefully stir in grapefruit sections.

Fish with Garlic Salsa

6 SERVINGS

2 *pounds cod, haddock, halibut or red*
  snapper fillets
2 *tablespoons margarine or butter, melted*
1 *tablespoon finely snipped cilantro, if*
  desired
½ *teaspoon salt*
1 *clove garlic, crushed*
Garlic Salsa (below)

If fish fillets are large, cut into 6 serving pieces. Place fish on rack in broiler pan. Mix margarine, cilantro, salt and garlic. Brush half of the mixture over fish. Set oven control to broil. Broil with tops about 4 inches from heat until light brown, about 6 minutes.

Turn fish carefully; brush with remaining margarine mixture. Broil until fish flakes very easily with fork, 4 to 6 minutes longer. Serve with Garlic Salsa; garnish with lime wedges, if desired.

GARLIC SALSA

3 *cloves garlic, crushed*
2 *medium tomatoes, finely chopped*
1 *medium onion, chopped (about ½ cup)*
1 *canned jalapeño pepper, seeded and*
  finely chopped
1 *tablespoon finely snipped fresh cilantro,*
  if desired
1 *tablespoon lemon juice*
½ *teaspoon dried oregano leaves*
1½ *teaspoons vegetable oil*

Heat all ingredients over medium heat, stirring occasionally, until hot and bubbly, about 5 minutes.

Oriental Fish Fillets with Bok Choy

½ pound bok choy
1 tablespoon sesame seed
1 tablespoon vegetable oil
1 bunch green onions (with tops), cut into
  2-inch pieces
1 small red pepper, cut into 1-inch pieces
1 pound fish fillets (cod, monkfish, orange
  roughy), cut into 1-inch pieces
½ cup chicken broth
½ teaspoon red pepper flakes
1 tablespoon cornstarch
1 tablespoon teriyaki sauce
Hot cooked rice

Remove leaves from bok choy; cut leaves into ½-inch strips. Cut stems into ¼-inch slices. Cook sesame seed in oil in 10-inch skillet over medium heat, stirring occasionally, until golden brown. Add bok choy stems, onions, red pepper, fish, broth and pepper flakes. Heat to boiling; reduce heat. Cover and simmer until fish is white, about 5 minutes.

Mix cornstarch and teriyaki sauce; gradually stir into skillet. Heat to boiling, stirring constantly. Boil and stir 1 minute. Stir in bok choy leaves until wilted. Serve over rice.

· 6 ·

SHELLFISH

Fried Soft-shell Crabs

12 soft-shell blue crabs
2 eggs
¼ cup milk
2 teaspoons salt
¾ cup all-purpose flour
¾ cup dry bread crumbs
Shortening

Have the fishmonger dress the crabs for eating. Rinse in cold water; drain.

Beat eggs, milk and salt until blended. Mix flour and crumbs. Dip crabs into egg mixture and coat with flour mixture.

Heat shortening (⅛ inch) in 10-inch skillet. Fry crabs in shortening over medium heat, turning carefully, until brown, 8 to 10 minutes. Serve with lemon wedges, if desired.

Maryland Crab Cakes

1 pound cooked Atlantic crabmeat, cartilage removed and flaked (2½ to
3 cups)
1½ cups soft white bread crumbs (without crusts)
2 tablespoons margarine or butter, melted
1 teaspoon dry mustard
½ teaspoon salt
⅛ teaspoon pepper
2 egg yolks, beaten
Vegetable oil

Mix all ingredients except oil. Shape into 4
patties. Refrigerate until firm.

Heat oil (1 inch) to 375°. Fry patties turning
once until golden brown on both sides, 4 to 5
minutes; drain.

Crab in Puff Pastry

½ package (17½-ounce size) frozen puff
pastry
2 tablespoons thinly sliced green onion
(with top)
2 tablespoons margarine or butter
2 tablespoons all-purpose flour
½ cup milk
½ cup whipping cream
1½ cups cooked crabmeat, lobster or
shrimp
½ cup sauvignon blanc or dry white wine
2 tablespoons snipped parsley
1 teaspoon finely shredded lemon peel
¼ teaspoon salt
⅛ teaspoon pepper

Thaw 1 sheet of puff pastry as directed on
package. Heat oven to 350°. Unfold pastry
and place on lightly floured surface. Roll into
10-inch square. Cut into halves; place one piece
on top of another. Roll to seal edges; cut crosswise into 4 equal pieces. Bake until golden
brown, about 20 minutes.

Cook onion in margarine in 2-quart saucepan
over low heat until tender. Stir in flour. Cook
over low heat, stirring constantly, until mixture is bubbly; remove from heat. Gradually
stir in milk and whipping cream. Heat to boiling, stirring constantly. Boil and stir 1 minute.
Stir in remaining ingredients; heat thoroughly.

Split each warm pastry horizontally with fork.
Spoon crab mixture over bottom halves; top
with remaining pastry halves. Garnish with
parsley, if desired.

Shrimp Veracruz

1 pound fresh or frozen shrimp
2 tablespoons margarine or butter
2 tablespoons vegetable oil
1 cup Casera Sauce (below)
1 tablespoon chopped fully cooked smoked
   ham

Peel shrimp. (If shrimp are frozen, do not thaw; peel under running cold water.) Make a shallow cut down back of each shrimp and wash out sand vein. Cut shrimp lengthwise almost into halves.

Heat margarine and oil in 10-inch skillet until hot. Cook and stir shrimp 1 minute. Add Casera Sauce and ham. Heat to boiling; reduce heat. Simmer uncovered until shrimp are pink, about 2 minutes. Garnish with snipped cilantro and lemon wedges, if desired.

CASERA SAUCE

2 medium tomatoes, finely chopped (about
   1 1/2 cups)
1 medium onion, chopped (about 1/2 cup)
1 small clove garlic, finely chopped
1 canned jalapeño pepper, seeded and
   finely chopped
1/2 teaspoon canned jalapeño pepper
   liquid
1 tablespoon finely snipped fresh cilantro
1 tablespoon lemon juice
1 1/2 teaspoons snipped fresh oregano
   leaves or 1/2 teaspoon dried oregano
   leaves
1 1/2 teaspoons vegetable oil

Mix all ingredients in glass or plastic bowl. Cover and refrigerate up to 7 days.

Shrimp Almond Ding

1 pound fresh or frozen raw shrimp
1 teaspoon cornstarch
½ teaspoon salt
½ teaspoon soy sauce
¼ teaspoon sesame oil
3 stalks celery
½ cup sliced canned bamboo shoots
½ cup canned water chestnuts
1 medium onion
2 tablespoons cornstarch
2 tablespoons cold water
2 tablespoons vegetable oil
½ cup blanched almonds
⅛ teaspoon salt
1 teaspoon finely chopped garlic
2 tablespoons vegetable oil
1 teaspoon salt
1 can (4 ounces) button mushrooms,
    drained
½ cup chicken broth
1 tablespoon dry white wine
½ cup frozen peas
2 tablespoons oyster sauce
2 green onions (with tops), chopped

Peel shrimp. (If shrimp are frozen, do not thaw; peel under running cold water.) Make a shallow cut lengthwise down back of each shrimp; wash out sand vein. Cut shrimp lengthwise into halves. Toss shrimp, 1 teaspoon cornstarch, ½ teaspoon salt, the soy sauce and sesame oil in glass or plastic bowl. Cover and refrigerate 20 minutes.

Cut celery, bamboo shoots and water chestnuts into ½-inch pieces. Cut onion into 18 pieces. Mix 2 tablespoons cornstarch and 2 tablespoons water.

Heat wok until 1 or 2 drops of water bubble and skitter when sprinkled in wok. Add 2 tablespoons vegetable oil; rotate wok to coat side. Add almonds; stir-fry until light brown, about 1 minute. Remove almonds from wok; drain on paper towel. Sprinkle with ⅛ teaspoon salt. Add onion pieces and garlic to wok; stir-fry until onion is tender. Add shrimp; stir-fry until shrimp are pink. Remove onion and shrimp from wok.

Add 2 tablespoons vegetable oil to wok; rotate to coat side. Add celery and 1 teaspoon salt; stir-fry 1 minute. Add bamboo shoots, water chestnuts and mushrooms; stir-fry 1 minute. Stir in chicken broth and wine; heat to boiling. Stir in cornstarch mixture; cook and stir until thickened, about 10 seconds. Stir in shrimp, onion pieces, peas and oyster sauce; heat to boiling. Garnish with almonds and green onions.

MICROWAVE REHEAT DIRECTIONS: Prepare Shrimp Almond Ding as directed except omit green onions; cover and refrigerate no longer than 24 hours. Store fried almonds in airtight container at room temperature no longer than 24 hours. Just before serving, prepare green onions. Cover shrimp mixture tightly and microwave on microwavable platter or bowl on high 4 minutes; stir. Cover and microwave until hot, about 4 minutes longer. Let stand covered 2 minutes. Garnish with almonds and green onions.

Shrimp with Feta Cheese

4 SERVINGS

1 large onion, chopped
2 cloves garlic, chopped
3 tablespoons olive or vegetable oil
½ cup dry white wine
1 tablespoon snipped fresh basil leaves
  or 1 teaspoon dried basil leaves
1 tablespoon snipped fresh oregano leaves
  or 1 teaspoon dried oregano leaves
½ teaspoon salt
Dash of ground red pepper
1 can (28 ounces) Italian plum tomatoes, drained and chopped
1 pound raw shrimp, shelled and deveined
2 tablespoons lemon juice
2 ounces feta cheese, crumbled
Snipped parsley

Cook and stir onion and garlic in oil in 10-inch skillet over medium heat until onion is tender. Stir in wine, basil, oregano, salt, red pepper and tomatoes. Heat to boiling; reduce heat. Simmer uncovered 20 minutes. Stir in shrimp and lemon juice. Cover and cook until shrimp are pink, 3 to 5 minutes. Sprinkle with cheese and parsley. Serve with hot cooked rice, if desired.

Following pages: Shrimp Almond Ding

Shrimp Cilantro

16 large fresh or frozen raw shrimp
1 medium onion, chopped (about ½ cup)
2 cloves garlic, finely chopped
2 tablespoons margarine or butter
2 tablespoons vegetable oil
2 tablespoons snipped fresh cilantro
Lemon slices

Peel shrimp. (If shrimp are frozen, do not thaw; peel under running cold water.) Make a shallow cut down back of each shrimp; wash out sand vein.

Cook and stir onion and garlic in margarine and oil in 10-inch skillet until tender. Add shrimp; cook 1 minute. Turn; cook until pink, about 2 minutes. (Do not overcook.) Sprinkle with cilantro. Pour pan juices over shrimp; garnish with lemon slices.

Grilled Texas Shrimp

¼ cup vegetable oil
¼ cup tequila
¼ cup red wine vinegar
2 tablespoons lime juice
1 tablespoon ground red chilies
½ teaspoon salt
2 cloves garlic, finely chopped
1 red bell pepper, finely chopped
24 large raw shrimp, peeled and deveined
  (leave tails intact)

Mix all ingredients except shrimp in shallow glass or plastic dish; stir in shrimp. Cover and refrigerate 1 hour.

Remove shrimp from marinade; reserve marinade. Thread 4 shrimp on each of six 8-inch metal skewers. Grill over medium coals, turning once, until shrimp are pink, 2 to 3 minutes on each side.

Heat marinade to boiling in nonaluminum saucepan; reduce heat to low. Simmer uncovered until bell pepper is tender, about 5 minutes. Serve with shrimp.

BROILED TEXAS SHRIMP: Set oven control to broil. Place skewered shrimp on rack in broiler pan. Broil with tops about 4 inches from heat, turning once, until shrimp are pink, 2 to 3 minutes on each side.

Shrimp Étouffée

1 pound fresh or frozen medium raw
*   shrimp (in shells)*
¼ cup margarine or butter
2 tablespoons all-purpose flour
1 medium onion, chopped (about ½ cup)
1 small green pepper, chopped (about
*   ½ cup)*
1 medium stalk celery, sliced (about
*   ½ cup)*
1 clove garlic, finely chopped
1 cup water
2 tablespoons snipped parsley
2 teaspoons lemon juice
½ teaspoon salt
¼ teaspoon pepper
⅛ to ¼ teaspoon red pepper sauce
Hot cooked rice

Peel shrimp. (If shrimp are frozen, do not thaw; peel under running cold water.) Make a shallow cut lengthwise down back of each shrimp; wash out sand vein.

Heat margarine in 3-quart saucepan over medium-low heat until melted. Stir in flour. Cook, stirring constantly, until bubbly and brown, about 6 minutes. Stir in onion, green pepper, celery and garlic. Cook and stir until vegetables are crisp-tender, about 5 minutes.

Stir in shrimp, water, parsley, lemon juice, salt, pepper and pepper sauce. Heat to boiling; reduce heat. Simmer uncovered, stirring occasionally, until shrimp are pink, about 5 minutes. Serve over rice.

CRAWFISH ÉTOUFFÉE: Substitute cleaned raw crawfish for the shrimp. (Sizes of crawfish vary depending on region and variety. Forty to 48 crawfish, each about 5 inches long, yield about 1 pound tail meat.)

Stir-fried Scallops and Pea Pods

4 SERVINGS

1 pound scallops
1 tablespoon packed brown sugar
1 tablespoon soy sauce
2 teaspoons cornstarch
6 slices bacon, cut into 1-inch pieces
6 green onions (with tops), cut into 1-inch
  pieces
1 can (8 ounces) sliced water chestnuts,
  drained
4 ounces fresh Chinese pea pods or
  1 package (6 ounces) frozen Chinese
  pea pods, thawed

If scallops are large, cut into halves. Toss scallops, brown sugar, soy sauce and cornstarch in bowl; cover and refrigerate 10 minutes.

Cook and stir bacon in 10-inch skillet or wok over medium heat until crisp. Drain, reserving 1 tablespoon fat in skillet; reserve bacon.

Cook and stir scallops, onions and water chestnuts in bacon fat over medium-high heat until scallops are white, about 7 minutes; stir in pea pods. Stir in bacon just before serving.

Broiled Ginger Scallops

3 SERVINGS

1 pound scallops
1/4 cup soy sauce
2 tablespoons finely chopped gingerroot
1/4 cup lemon juice
2 tablespoons vegetable oil
1 tablespoon honey

If scallops are large, cut into halves. Arrange scallops in single layer in square baking dish, 8 × 8 × 2 inches. Heat soy sauce to boiling. Add gingerroot; reduce heat. Simmer uncovered 5 minutes. Stir in remaining ingredients; pour over scallops. Cover and refrigerate, stirring occasionally, 2 hours.

Set oven control to broil. Remove scallops from marinade with slotted spoon. Arrange in single layer on rack in broiler pan. Broil with tops 3 to 4 inches from heat until opaque in center, about 5 minutes.

Steamed Clams with Sausage

4 SERVINGS

2 pounds very small clams
1 large onion, thinly sliced
3 cloves garlic, chopped
1 small red or green pepper, cut into
  1-inch pieces
1/2 teaspoon paprika
1/8 teaspoon crushed red pepper
2 tablespoons olive or vegetable oil
1/2 cup dry white wine
1/2 cup chopped fully cooked smoked ham
1 package (5 ounces) unsliced pepper-
  oni, chopped
1 can (16 ounces) whole tomatoes (with
  liquid)
2 bay leaves

Scrub clams with a stiff brush under running cold water.

Cook and stir onion, garlic, red pepper pieces, paprika and crushed red pepper in oil in Dutch oven over medium heat until onion is tender. Stir in remaining ingredients except clams; break up tomatoes with fork. Heat to boiling; reduce heat. Simmer uncovered 15 minutes.

Add clams to vegetable mixture. Cover and simmer 20 minutes. (Do not lift cover or stir.) Remove bay leaves and any unopened clams; discard. Serve with French bread, if desired.

Scalloped Oysters

4 SERVINGS

1 pint shucked select or large oysters,
  undrained
1/2 to 3/4 cup half-and-half
3 cups soft bread crumbs
1/2 cup margarine or butter, melted
2 teaspoons celery seed
1 teaspoon salt
1/4 teaspoon pepper

Arrange oysters in greased rectangular baking dish, 12 × 7½ × 2 inches. Pour about ¼ cup of the half-and-half over oysters.

Mix remaining ingredients except half-and-half; sprinkle over oysters. Top with remaining half-and-half (liquid should come about ¾ of the way up on oysters). Sprinkle with paprika, if desired. Bake uncovered in 375° oven until hot, 30 to 40 minutes.

Lobster with Chinese Vegetables

1½ pounds frozen lobster tails
1 package (6 ounces) frozen Chinese pea
    pods
3 medium stalks bok choy
2 tablespoons vegetable oil
2 cloves garlic, finely chopped
2 thin slices gingerroot, crushed
1 can (8 ounces) water chestnuts, drained
    and thinly sliced
1 can (8 ounces) bamboo shoots, drained
4 ounces mushrooms, sliced
1 can (10¾ ounces) condensed chicken
    broth
2 tablespoons cornstarch
2 tablespoons soy sauce
1 teaspoon salt
1 teaspoon sugar
¼ teaspoon white pepper
2 green onions, thinly sliced
Hot cooked rice

Cook lobster tails as directed on package; drain. Cut away thin undershell (covering meat of lobster) with kitchen scissors. Remove meat; cut into 1-inch pieces.

Rinse pea pods under running cold water to separate; drain. Separate leaves from bok choy stems; reserve leaves. Cut stems into ¼-inch slices. Heat oil in 12-inch skillet, Dutch oven or wok until hot. Cook and stir garlic and gingerroot over medium heat until brown. Add pea pods, bok choy stems, water chestnuts, bamboo shoots and mushrooms. Cook and stir over medium heat 2 minutes. Stir in ¾ cup of the chicken broth; reduce heat. Cover and simmer 1 minute.

Mix remaining chicken broth, the cornstarch, soy sauce, salt, sugar and white pepper; stir into vegetable mixture. Cook and stir until thickened, about 30 seconds. Tear bok choy leaves into bite-size pieces; add leaves and lobster to vegetable mixture. Heat until hot. Garnish with green onions; serve with rice.

Rice and Seafood (Paella)

8 SERVINGS

16 mussels (in shells)
8 clams (in shells)
1 cup uncooked regular rice
1/4 cup olive or vegetable oil
2 chorizo sausages, cooked and sliced
1 cup chicken broth
1 cup clam juice
1 cup green peas
1/2 cup chopped carrots
Dash of ground saffron
8 fresh or frozen raw shrimp (in shells)

Scrub mussels and clams with stiff brush under running cold water. Cook and stir rice in oil in 4-quart Dutch oven until golden brown. Stir in chorizo sausages, chicken broth, clam juice, peas, carrots and saffron. Place remaining ingredients on top of rice mixture. Heat to boiling; reduce heat. Cover and simmer 20 minutes. (Do not lift cover or stir.) Remove and discard any unopened mussels or clams. Garnish with snipped fresh cilantro and lemon wedges, if desired.

Seafood Chilaquiles Casserole

6 SERVINGS

1/2 cup vegetable oil
10 flour or corn tortillas (6 to 7 inches in diameter), cut into 1/2-inch strips
1/2 cup sliced green onions (with tops)
1/4 cup margarine or butter
1/4 cup all-purpose flour
1/2 teaspoon salt
1/4 teaspoon pepper
2 cups half-and-half
1 canned chipotle chili in adobo sauce, finely chopped
1 pound bay scallops
1 pound shelled medium raw shrimp
4 slices bacon, crisply cooked and crumbled

Heat oil in 10-inch skillet until hot. Cook tortilla strips in oil until light golden brown, 30 to 60 seconds; drain and reserve.

Cook onions in margarine in 3-quart saucepan over low heat until tender; stir in flour, salt and pepper. Cook, stirring constantly, until mixture is bubbly. Remove from heat; stir in half-and-half. Heat to boiling, stirring constantly. Boil and stir 1 minute; reduce heat. Stir in remaining ingredients except bacon. Cook over medium heat, stirring frequently, just until shrimp are pink, about 9 minutes.

Heat oven to 350°. Layer half of the tortilla strips in bottom of greased 3-quart casserole; top with half of the seafood mixture. Repeat with remaining tortilla strips and seafood mixture; top with bacon. Bake until hot, 15 to 20 minutes.

Following pages: Lobster with Chinese Vegetables

RED SPOON TIPS

The Smart Shopper's Guide to Fresh Fish

"The fresher the better" is truer of fish than probably any other food, but how can you tell fresh from less-than-fresh? The first thing a smart fish shopper should do is take a deep breath. Any fish market worth its salt will smell of fresh sea air; it should smell faintly of the sea and nothing else—no iodine, no ammonia, no "fishy" overtones.

Next, look for a thermometer in the display case. It should read 33°F, no more and no less. But beyond these basic rules, there are a couple of clues that can help you avoid seafood that is past its prime. Judging freshness in fish in any form depends on common sense and a good sense of smell.

How Fresh and How Much?

Fresh fish is sold in a variety of forms ranging from-right-from-the-water to pan-ready. Whole fish, also called round fish, is just as complete as when it was swimming, with head, tail, gills and entrails intact. Drawn fish is the entire fish, but it has been eviscerated, with the intestines and sometimes the gills removed. The freshness of these two forms is easy to gauge at a glance. Take a good look at the eyes. They should be clear, shiny and bulging. Dull, opaque or sunken eyes, or those with a great deal of redness, indicate fish that are over the hill or have been roughly treated. (Red snapper eyes are naturally red; just be sure they're also clear and bulging.) Gills should be pink or red, not brown and shaggy. Take a sniff if you're not sure. Any strong smell is an age giveaway. Buy about one pound of whole fish per serving, about ¾ pound of drawn (eviscerated).

Dressed fish has been scaled as well as gutted and may or may not have lost its head, tail and fins. Its flesh should be firm, the skin shiny and moist. Buy about ½ pound of dressed fish per serving.

Fillets are the two boneless (or nearly so) slabs of flesh removed from both sides of the backbone. When they are left attached to each other, they're known as butterfly fillets. Fillets are a little more difficult to judge for freshness. They should be moist-looking and shiny, but only your nose knows for sure. If thin fillets look opaque instead of translucent, chances are they've been frozen and thawed. Avoid them if you're paying high prices for fresh fish. Allow about ¼ pound per serving of filleted fish.

Steaks are generally cut from large, thick fish such as salmon, swordfish and tuna. They are cross-cut from ½ to 1½ inches thick from dressed fish and often contain small bones. Look for the same characteristics as in fresh fillets and buy about ⅓ pound fish steak per serving.

When You Buy Frozen

Check that the package is not ripped or damaged and that the fish is solidly frozen. It should have no odor. Cook it still frozen for best texture and taste, or thaw slowly in the refrigerator, allowing about 18 hours per pound. The microwave oven is a real timesaver here; follow the manufacturer's instructions. Don't keep frozen fish for longer than 2 months; once thawed, it should be used immediately.

How to Keep Fresh Fish Fresh

Never store an ungutted fish. If your neighbor offers you some surplus catch-of-the-day, ask him if it's been drawn and scaled. If not, and if you don't want to do it yourself, tell him thanks, but no thanks. Undrawn fish deteriorates very quickly. Because fish are cold-blooded, changes in temperature affect them more. An increase of 10°F in storage temperature will double the rate of deterioration.

Always make the fish store your last stop on the way home. Once you get home, refrigerate your fish immediately. If you're not using it within an hour or two, zip it into a plastic bag and bury it in ice. A whole, drawn fish should have ice packed into its cavity as well.

How to Cook It

You can cook fish just about any way you like. It's naturally tender since it has far less connective tissue than meat. In fact, there are even fish that have no bones— only cartilage—shark and sturgeon to name two. Cooking brings out or enhances flavor and improves texture, so long as it's not overdone.

Fish fall into two categories: lean and fatty, and that's what determines the best cooking method for each type of fish. Be aware, though, that even so-called fatty fish have less fat than some meats and that their Omega-3 oils have been credited with lowering human cholesterol levels.

Broil, bake and plank (literally, cook on a wooden board) fatty fish like salmon, mackerel, pompano and whitefish; steam or poach lean fish like flounder, sole, cod, halibut, grouper, snapper, swordfish, bass and perch. Both lean and fatty fish can be pan fried or deep fried.

The microwave oven and the grill are also wonderful ways to cook fish. The microwave is especially gentle to the delicate flesh, and the grill adds great flavor, even to lean fish when properly basted.

An intriguing way to cook and serve many kinds of fish is known as *en papillote*. (See Pompano en Papillote, page 64.) The fish and appropriate seasonings are carefully folded in a packet of parchment or aluminum foil, and baked in the oven. The packets are brought intact to the table where they are slit open to release fragrant bouquets of steam—a dramatic and savory presentation that concentrates flavor and aromas but is astoundingly easy to make.

Whatever method you use, don't overdo it; fish becomes dry and bland when overcooked. So how do you tell when it's done? You can use an instant-read thermometer; the traditional recommended reading is 160°F. Most recipes read "until fish flakes easily." What does that really mean? Pull gently on the edge of a piece of cooked fish with the tip of a fork; you'll see that the flesh separates into small, well-defined segments that look a little like shingles or roof tiles . . . or flakes.

Shellfish

Shrimp, crab and lobster were once synonymous with luxury dining. Although often still expensive, they are much more readily available and have become popular throughout the country. One reason is their ease of preparation. Oysters, clams and mussels cook in mere minutes.

Lobsters are sold either live or cooked. To be sure a lobster is alive—if its feelers and legs aren't visibly waving—hold it upside down and run a fingernail quickly and firmly up the underside of the tail. If this doesn't cause the tail to curl up sharply, the animal is either dead or so near to it you're better off without it. The large pincer claws are wrapped with sturdy rubber bands or plugged with small pieces of wood to avoid painful pinches. Holding the lobster by the back will keep even the small claws from reaching your hands.

Because they are so perishable, hard-shell crabs are sold live only near the coast where they are caught. Soft-shell crabs (simply blue crabs that have shed their hard shells to accommodate growth) are available in spring and early summer. Your fishmonger will clean them and get them ready for you to coat with flour, bread crumbs or cornmeal and then panfry or deep fry. Eat them, soft shells and all, with a squeeze of lemon juice or with tartar sauce.

Hard-shell crabs and lobsters are most often steamed or simmered, and cooking them is the easy part. Getting the succulent meat out of the shells is one of life's most enjoyable chores. You'll need a nutcracker or pliers and a nut pick or small fork—and a bib or at least plenty of napkins.

FOR HARD-SHELL CRAB: On the underside is a small tail flap; lift it up and tear it off. Turn the crab right side up and pry up and lift off the top shell. Discard the gray-white, feathery gills. Break off the large claws and set aside. Twist off the legs, gently but firmly pulling any attached meat from inside the shell. Break the claws at the joints and use a nutcracker to crack the shell. Extract meat with a nutpick or small fork. Break the body in half with your hands or cut in half with a large knife or cleaver. Pick out meat from deep pockets.

FOR LOBSTER: Put the cooked lobster on its back on several layers of newspaper to catch the water that will run out. Cut the lobster in half lengthwise with a heavy, sharp knife. Spread the halves so that you can remove the stomach, a dark soft substance behind the head, and the dark intestinal vein that runs down the center of the tail. Don't discard the green tomalley or the orange coral roe, if there is any; both are delicacies and can be eaten or used to flavor lobster butter. The tail meat can be lifted out with a fork. Crack the claws with a nutcracker or pliers and remove meat with a nutpick or small fork. Serious lobster lovers will tear off the small legs and suck and squeeze meat from them with their teeth. The tail flippers contain petal-thin sheets of the most delicate meat for those with the patience to remove it carefully. Serve hot lobster with lemon slices and melted butter. Cold lobster is better with mayonnaise.

Shrimp

Your nose is more reliable than your eyes when choosing fresh shrimp. There are so many varieties with such a wide range of colors that looks can be deceiving: Gray or brownish shrimp can be fresher than pink ones. Any ammonia-like smell indicates shrimp that is best avoided. Shrimp can be purchased cooked or raw (often it has been frozen at sea, then thawed), shelled or not, but it is almost always headless. Look for tightly fitting shells and firm texture.

To clean and shell shrimp, whether cooked or raw, grasp the legs and pull them off. That will release the underside of the shell, which can then be peeled off. With the tip of a knife, make a shallow cut down the back and remove the dark vein under running water. Shrimp are commonly graded small, medium and large, running about 30, 24 and 18 shrimp per pound, respectively. Tiny shrimp generally come from very cold waters and are very flavorful. The jumbo ones are especially delicious when simply split down the back, deveined and cooked in their shells on a charcoal grill.

Clams and Mussels

Hard-shell clams, known variously as little-necks, cherry-stones and quahogs, will open on their own when cooked, as will soft-shell steamers and mussels. Discard any broken or open shells before cooking.

Scrub the shells and pull beards from mussels. Soak in cool water for at least half an hour or in the refrigerator overnight to get rid of excess sand that might be inside. Discard any clam or mussel that doesn't open during cooking.

Oysters

Scrub shells thoroughly and open with a sturdy knife or the point of a can opener. When using oysters in Oysters Rockefeller, in an oyster stew or fried, you can open them easily in the microwave oven: Arrange six at a time in a circle, with hinges facing the rim of a microwavable plate lined with microwavable paper toweling. Cover tightly and microwave on high for 1 to 1½ minutes, removing the oysters as they open and cutting the meat away from both shell halves. Although it is undeniable that oysters shucked just before eating have the best taste, fresh oysters are also available conveniently shucked. When buying shucked oysters, be sure they're plump and sweet-smelling and that the liquid in which they're sitting is clear.

Scallops

Both bay (small) and sea (large) scallops are almost never sold live in the shell, although you may find them with their coral or pink roe still attached. If you do, buy them immediately for a rare culinary treat. In general, look for scallops that are translucent in clear liquid. Scallops are quite rich and, since there is no waste, ¼ pound will be an ample serving. Bread them and deep-fry them, or sauté them and serve with browned butter and lemon wedges. As with fin fish, avoid overcooking. All shellfish become tough and flavorless when overcooked.

COOKING METHODS

TYPE OF SEAFOOD/FISH	FORM READILY AVAILABLE	FAT OR LEAN	RECOMMENDED COOKING METHOD
Bass	whole, drawn, fillets	lean	bake, broil, grill, panfry
Bluefish	whole, drawn, fillets	lean	bake, broil, grill
Catfish	whole, dressed, skinned, steaks, fillets	lean	bake, broil, grill, panfry
Clams	in the shell, shucked	lean	bake, panfry, steamed
Cod	drawn, dressed steaks, fillets	lean	bake, grill, poach
Crab, Dungeness, hard-shell, soft-shell	live, cooked	lean	cook in liquid
Flounder (others called sole: gray, lemon, rex)	whole, dressed, fillets	lean	bake, broil, grill, panfry, poach
Grouper	whole, drawn, dressed, steaks, fillets	lean	bake, panfry, poach
Haddock	drawn, fillets	lean	bake, broil, grill, panfry, poach
Hake	whole, drawn, dressed, fillets	lean	bake, broil, grill, panfry, poach
Halibut	dressed, steaks	lean	bake, broil, grill, panfry, poach
Herring, sea	whole	fat	bake, broil, panfry, pickle in brine, smoke
Lobster	live, cooked	lean	bake, cook in liquid
Mackerel	whole, drawn, fillets	fat	bake, broil, panfry, poach
Mullet	whole, fillets	lean	bake, broil, panfry, cook in liquid

TYPE OF SEAFOOD/FISH	FORM READILY AVAILABLE	FAT OR LEAN	RECOMMENDED COOKING METHOD
Mussels	in the shell	lean	bake, panfry, steamed
Oysters	in the shell, shucked	lean	bake, panfry, poach, steamed
Pike, northern, walleye	whole, dressed, fillets	lean	bake, broil, grill, panfry
Pollack	drawn, dressed steaks, fillets	lean	bake, broil, grill, panfry, poach
Porgy (scup)	whole, dressed	lean	panfry
Red snapper	drawn, dressed steaks, fillets	lean	bake, broil, grill, panfry, poach
Rockfish	dressed, fillets	lean	bake, broil, grill, panfry, poach
Salmon	drawn, dressed steaks, fillets	fat	bake, broil, grill, panfry, poach, smoke
Scallops	shucked	lean	bake, broil, panfry, poach
Sea bass	whole, dressed, fillets	lean	bake, broil, poach
Shad	whole, drawn, fillets	fat	bake, broil, panfry
Shrimp	headless in the shell, cooked	lean	bake, broil, grill, panfry, cook in liquid
Smelt	whole, drawn	lean	deep fry, panfry
Sole, Dover	drawn, dressed, fillets	lean	bake, broil, panfry, poach
Tuna, albacore, bluefin, bonito	whole (if small), steaks	lean	bake, broil, grill, poach
Trout, lake	drawn, dressed, fillets	fat	bake, broil, grill, smoke
Trout, sea (weakfish)	whole, drawn, dressed, fillets	lean	bake, broil, grill, panfry
Whitefish	whole, drawn, dressed, fillets	fat	bake, poach

Source: General Mills, Inc.

SAUCES

Fish is never better than when it is cooked simply, whether grilled, broiled, poached or sautéed. Sometimes a squeeze of fresh lemon is all that is needed to bring out the brilliance of seafood, but there are times when the flavor of a homemade sauce adds just the right note of luxury and comfort. The sauces that follow run the gamut from classic velouté to a spicy-rich mayonnaise flavored with chipotle chilies and are just about perfect with cold poached fish. There is something here for every taste. Capers add a mediterranean touch, and tartar sauce is as American as the Fourth of July.

Note: If they are not to be served directly after preparing, keep butter-based sauces warm on very low heat.

Velouté Sauce

ABOUT 1 CUP

2 tablespoons margarine or butter
2 tablespoons all-purpose flour
1 cup chicken broth
¼ teaspoon salt
⅛ teaspoon pepper
⅛ teaspoon ground nutmeg

Heat margarine in 1½-quart saucepan over low heat until melted. Stir in flour. Cook over low heat, stirring constantly, until mixture is smooth and bubbly; remove from heat. Stir in broth. Heat to boiling, stirring constantly. Boil and stir 1 minute. Stir in remaining ingredients.

ALLEMANDE SAUCE: Heat margarine until melted as directed; reserve. Mix flour, salt, pepper and nutmeg in 1½-quart saucepan. Mix broth and 1 egg yolk until blended; stir into flour mixture. Heat to boiling, stirring constantly. Boil and stir 1 minute; remove from heat. Stir in margarine, 2 tablespoons half-and-half and 1 teaspoon lemon juice.

ALMOND VELVET SAUCE: Prepare Velouté Sauce. Just before serving, stir in ¼ cup toasted slivered almonds.

MORNAY SAUCE: Prepare Velouté Sauce except substitute ½ cup half-and-half for ½ cup of the chicken broth. After boiling and stirring 1 minute, stir in ⅛ teaspoon ground red pepper and ½ cup grated Parmesan or shredded Swiss cheese until melted.

Dill Sauce

1 CUP

2 tablespoons margarine or butter
2 tablespoons all-purpose flour
1 teaspoon snipped fresh dill or ½ teaspoon dried dill weed
¼ teaspoon salt
⅛ teaspoon pepper
Dash ground nutmeg
1 cup milk

Heat margarine in 1½-quart saucepan over low heat until melted. Stir in flour, dill, salt, pepper and nutmeg. Cook over low heat, stirring constantly, until mixture is smooth and bubbly; remove from heat. Stir in milk. Heat to boiling, stirring constantly. Boil and stir 1 minute.

THIN DILL SAUCE: Decrease margarine to 1 tablespoon and flour to 1 tablespoon.

Avocado Sauce

ABOUT ¾ CUP

1 small avocado, peeled and cut up
⅓ cup dairy sour cream
1 teaspoon lemon juice
¼ teaspoon salt
Few drops red pepper sauce

Beat all ingredients with hand beater until smooth.

Caper Sauce

ABOUT ⅓ CUP

1 lemon
¼ cup capers, drained
1 tablespoon snipped parsley
1 tablespoon margarine or butter
¼ teaspoon salt

Pare and section lemon; remove seeds. Chop lemon; mix with remaining ingredients. Heat until hot.

Tartar Sauce

ABOUT 1 CUP

1 cup mayonnaise or salad dressing
2 tablespoons finely chopped dill pickle
1 tablespoon snipped parsley
2 teaspoons chopped pimiento
1 teaspoon grated onion

Mix all ingredients; cover and refrigerate until chilled.

Lime Butter Sauce

¾ CUP

2 egg yolks
1 tablespoon lime juice
½ cup firm butter*
½ teaspoon grated lime peel

Stir egg yolks and lime juice vigorously in 1½-quart saucepan. Add ¼ cup of the butter. Heat over very low heat, stirring constantly, until butter is melted.

Add remaining butter. Continue heating, stirring vigorously, until butter is melted and sauce is thickened. (Be sure butter melts slowly so that sauce will thicken without curdling.) Stir in lime peel. Serve hot or at room temperature. Cover and refrigerate remaining sauce.

*Margarine not recommended.

Lemon Butter Sauce

½ cup butter*
1 tablespoon lemon juice
1 tablespoon snipped parsley
¼ teaspoon red pepper sauce

Heat all ingredients over low heat, stirring constantly, until butter is melted.

*Margarine not recommended.

Chipotle Mayonnaise

ABOUT 1 CUP

½ cup mayonnaise
½ cup dairy sour cream
¼ teaspoon snipped fresh oregano leaves
  or ⅛ teaspoon dried oregano leaves,
  if desired
2 canned chipotle chilies in adobo sauce,
  finely chopped

Mix all ingredients. Cover and refrigerate until chilled, about 1 hour.

How to Serve a Whole Fish

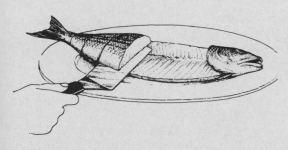

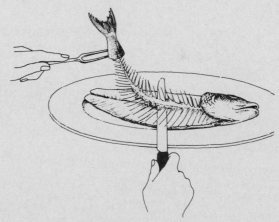

Cut the top side of fish into serving pieces, just down to the bone. Carefully remove pieces from the rib bone. Remove stuffing, if any.

Remove rib bones; cut the lower section into serving pieces.

How to Fillet a Fish Before Cooking

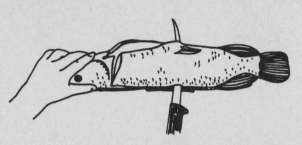

Turn fish on its side; make a cut behind the gills straight down to the backbone. Turn the knife blade flat; cut along the backbone almost to tail. (Except for tail portion, top fillet will be separated from the rest of the fish with the narrow rib cage still attached.)

Without removing knife, lift the fillet away from backbone and entrails and flip it to the right so that the flesh side is on top and the skin side on the bottom. Cut the fillet away from the skin in one piece by sliding the knife between the skin and the flesh. Use a sawing motion and press the knife blade close to the skin to remove as much flesh as possible.

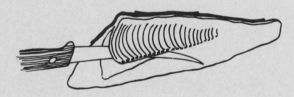

Cut the rib cage from the fillet. Turn the fish over and repeat the above steps to remove the second fillet.

Tip: If the fillets are of uneven thickness, turn the thin ends under the fillets and bake for even cooking. Use this method for any kind of fish fillets whose tail ends are thinner than the head ends.

INDEX

Allemande Sauce, 104
Almond Velvet Sauce, 105
Anchovy-Garlic Dip, 12
Appetizers and first courses,
  Caviar Canapés, 16
  Crab and Avocado Cocktail, 12
  Crabmeat Puffs, 17
  Dip, Anchovy-Garlic, 12
  Fish en Escabeche, 13
  Fish, Smoked, 16
  Melon and Smoked Salmon, 9
  Oysters Rockefeller, 8
  Oysters, Stuffed, 8
  Salmon Pinwheels, 9
  Scallops, Parsley, 7
  Squid, Fried, 7
  Tuna Salsa, Chunky, 13
Avocado
  Crab and, Cocktail, 12
  Sandwiches, Club, Shrimp and, 54
  Sauce, 106

Baked Fish with Grapefruit Sauce, 78–79
Baked Red Snapper, 69
Bisque, Clam, 27
Broiled Ginger Scallops, 90

Caper Sauce, 106
Carolina Crabmeat Soup, 28
Casserole, Crab Scramble, 42
Casserole, Seafood Chilaquiles, 93
Catfish, Southern-fried, 61
Caviar Canapés, 16
Chilled Shrimp, Pea Pods and Bean Curd,
  45
Chipotle Mayonnaise, 107
Chowder
  Fish and Corn, 21
  Fish, Hearty, 22
  Manhattan Clam, 26
  New England, 23
  Oyster and Vegetable, 27
  Salmon, Dilled, 21
Chunky Tuna Salsa, 13
Clam(s)
  Bisque, 27
  preparing, 100–101
  Steamed, with Sausage, 91
Cocktail Sauce, 105
Cod and Vegetable Bake, 74
Cooking methods, 102–103
Corn Chowder, Fish and, 21

Crab(s)
  Cakes, Maryland, 82
  Casserole, Scramble, 42
  Cocktail, Avocado and, 12
  Custards, Herbed, 39
  Frittata, 42
  Hard-shell, 99–100
  Louis, 44–45
  in Puff Pastry, 82
  Puffs, 17
  Soft-shell, buying and eating, 99
  Soft-shell, Fried, 81
  Soup, Carolina, 28
Creamy Fish Soup with Garlic Toast,
  23

Dill Sauce, 105
Dilled Salmon Chowder, 21
Dip, Anchovy-Garlic, 12
Drawn fish, 97
Dressed fish, 97

Egg(s)
  Casserole, Crab Scramble, 42
  Foo Yung, Shrimp, 35
  Frittata, Crabmeat, 42
  Pie, Salmon Impossible, 33
  Pie, Tuna Impossible, 33
  Sandwiches, Curried, and Shrimp, 54
  Scrambled, with Smoked Salmon, 33
  Shrimp, Stir-fried, with, 34
En Papillote cooking method, 99

Fillets, buying, 97–98
Fish. *See also* specific fish
  Baked, with Grapefruit Sauce, 78–79
  Chowder, and Corn, 21
  cooking, 98–99
  cooking methods, 5–6, 102–103
  filleting, 108
  freshness of, 97–98
  frozen, buying, 98
  with Garlic Salsa, 79
  Ginger-sauced, 68
  keeping fresh, 98
  Oriental, Fillets with Bok Choy, 80
  seasonings, 6
  serving whole fish, 108
  Shopper's Guide to, 97
  steaks, buying, 98
  Steamed, 75
  Stir-fried, with Pea Pods, 78

Fried Soft-shell Crabs, 81
Fried Squid, 7

Garlic Dip, Anchovy-, 12
Ginger-sauced Fish, 68
Gumbo, Shrimp, 29

Halibut, Baked, with Cilantro Pesto, 71
Hard-shell crab, buying, 99
Hard-shell crab, eating, 99–100
Hearty Fish Chowder, 22
Herbed Crab Custards, 39
Herring Salad, 52
Hot and Sour Fish Soup, 22

Lemon Butter Sauce, 106
Lime Butter Sauce, 107
Lobster(s)
  buying, 99
  with Chinese Vegetables, 92
  cooking, 99
  preparing and eating, 100

Manhattan Clam Chowder, 26
Maryland Crab Cakes, 82
Mayonnaise, Chipotle, 107
Mediterranean Fish Soup, 26
Melon and Smoked Salmon, 9
Microwave oven, 99
Mornay Sauce, 105
Mussels, preparing, 100–101
Mustard Sauce, 106

New England Chowder, 23

Omelet, Smoked Fish, 34
Orange Almond Trout, 61
Oriental Fish Fillets with Bok Choy, 80
Oriental Oyster Stew, 28
Oyster(s)
  Chowder, and Vegetable, 27
  microwaving, 101
  preparing, 101
  Rockefeller, 8
  Scalloped, 91
  Stew, Oriental, 28
  Stuffed, 8

Paella (Rice and Seafood), 93
Parsley Scallops, 7
Pompano en Papillote, 64–65

Red Snapper, Baked, 69
Red Snapper, Wild Rice-stuffed, 74–75
Rice and Seafood (Paella), 93

Salad(s)
  Crab Louis, 44–45
  Herring, 52

Salmon and Grapefruit, 50
Salmon, Grilled, 50
Salmon-Squash, 51
Seafood
  with Dill Dressing, 46
  Greek, 44
  in Pita, 55
  -Wild Rice, 47
Scallop, Warm, 47
Shrimp, Marinated, 43
Shrimp, Pea Pods and Bean Curd, Chilled, 45
Tuna
  Layered, 53
  Sandwiches, Cobb Salad, 58
  and Tomato, 53
Salmon. *See also* Smoked Salmon
  Chowder, Dilled, 21
  with Creamy Cucumber Salsa, 70
  Impossible Pie, 33
  Pinwheels, 9
  Salad, and Grapefruit, 50
  Salad, Grilled, 50
  Steaks, Baked, 71
  -Wild Rice Soup, 20
Sandwiches
  Egg and Shrimp, Curried, 54
  Seafood, Broiled, 55
  Seafood Salad in Pita, 55
  Shrimp and Avocado Club, 54
  Tuna
    Cobb Salad, 58
    Patty, 59
    Tunawiches, 58
Sauces
  Allemande, 104
  Almond Velvet, 105
  Avocado, 106
  Caper, 106
  Cocktail, 105
  Dill, 105
  Lemon Butter, 106
  Lime Butter, 107
  Mayonnaise, Chipotle, 107
  Mornay, 105
  Mustard, 106
  Tartar, 107
  Velouté, 104
Scalloped Oysters, 91
Scallop(s)
  buying and preparing, 101
  Ginger, Broiled, 90
  Parsley, 7
  Salad, Warm, 47
  Stir-fried, and Pea Pods, 90
Scrambled Eggs with Smoked Salmon, 33
Sea Bass in Cilantro, 69
Seafood,
  Chilaquiles Casserole, 93

Seafood (*cont.*)
  Rice and, (Paella), 93
  -Wild Rice Salad, 47
Shellfish. *See also* specific shellfish
  buying, 99
  cooking methods, 6, 102–103
Shrimp
  Almond Ding, 84–85
  buying and preparing, 100
  Chilled, Pea Pods and Bean Curd, 45
  Cilantro, 88
  Egg Foo Yung, 35
  Etouffée, 89
  with Feta Cheese, 85
  Grilled Texas, 88
  Gumbo, 29
  Salad, Marinated, 43
  Sandwiches, Club, and Avocado, 54
  Sandwiches, Curried Egg and, 54
  Soufflé, 38–39
  Stir-fried, with Eggs, 34
  Veracruz, 83
Smoked Fish Appetizers, 16
Smoked Fish Omelet, 34
Smoked Salmon
  Melon and, 9
  Pinwheels, 9
  Scrambled Eggs with, 33
  Soufflé, and Broccoli, 32
Soft-shell crabs, buying and eating, 99
Sole with Red Grapes, 60
Soufflé, Shrimp, 38–39
Soufflé, Smoked Salmon and Broccoli,
    32
Soup
  Crabmeat, Carolina, 28
  Creamy Fish, with Garlic Toast, 23

Hot and Sour Fish, 22
Mediterranean Fish, 26
Salmon-Wild Rice, 20
Southern-fried Catfish, 61
Squid, Fried, 7
Steaks, 98
Steamed Clams with Sausage, 91
Steamed Fish, 75
Stew, Oriental Oyster, 28
Stir-fried
  Fish with Pea Pods, 78
  Scallops and Pea Pods, 90
  Shrimp with Eggs, 34
Stuffed Oysters, 8

Tartar Sauce, 107
Trout with Cabbage and Apples, 64
Trout, Orange Almond, 61
Tuna
  Salad, Layered, 53
  Salad, and Tomato, 53
  Salsa, Chunky, 13
  Sandwiches, Cobb Salad, 58
  Sandwiches, Patty, 59
  Tunawiches, 58

Vegetable(s)
  Bake, Cod and, 74
  Chinese, Lobster with, 92
  Chowder, Oyster and, 27
Velouté Sauce, 104

Whole fish, serving, 108
Wild Rice
  Salad, Seafood-, 47
  Soup, Salmon-, 20
  -stuffed Red Snapper, 74–75

V.P., Publisher: Anne M. Zeman
Project Editor: Rebecca W. Atwater
Editorial Assistant: Rachel A. Simon
Photographer: Anthony Johnson
Food Stylist: Paul Grimes
Designers: Patricia Fabricant, Frederick J. Latasa
Production Manager: Lessley Davis
Production Editor: Kimberly Ebert